"*Paleo Sweets and Treats* is not only a gorgeous book, but a book that will talk any nonpaleo eater into being a believer. Heather uses creative cooking and baking techniques to bring desserts to your table in a whole new way. Her recipes are also simple and easy to create over and over. You will not be disappointed in this book!"

—Juli of PaleOMG.com and author of *OMG that's Paleo?*

"If your family is struggling to get onto the grain-free whole foods bandwagon because traditional sweets are calling your name, then *Paleo Sweets and Treats* may be just the thing you need to get onboard."

—Stacy, Paleo Parents, http://paleoparents.com

"As a Paleo mom, I am so glad to have this book on my shelf. Although I love to cook, I am not much of a baker. *Paleo Sweets and Treats* will be my go-to guide for all birthday parties and special occasions. This book is filled with creative and delicious recipes that emphasize seasonal, whole ingredients. They will leave your guests loaded with nutrients and questioning if the desserts were really Paleo. If you enjoy sweets and also care about your health, this book is for you!"

—Arsy Vartanian, author of *Paleo Slow Cooker* (Race Point, 2013) and rubiesandradishes.com

© 2013 Fair Winds Press
Text © 2013 Heather Connell
Photography © Fair Winds Press

First published in the USA in 2013 by
Fair Winds Press, a member of
Quayside Publishing Group
100 Cummings Center
Suite 406-L
Beverly, MA 01915-6101

www.fairwindspress.com
Visit www.QuarrySPOON.com and help us celebrate food and culture one spoonful at a time!

17 16 15 14 13   1 2 3 4 5

ISBN: 978-1-59233-556-5

Digital edition published in 2013
eISBN: 978-1-61058-913-0

Library of Congress Cataloging-in-Publication Data

Connell, Heather.
  Paleo sweets & treats : seasonally-inspired desserts that let you have your cake and
your paleo lifestyle, too / Heather Connell.
    pages cm
  Includes bibliographical references and index.
  ISBN 978-1-59233-556-5 (alk. paper)
 1. Desserts. 2. Cake. 3. Gluten-free diet--Recipes. I. Title. II. Title: Paleo sweets
and treats. III. Title: Seasonally-inspired desserts that let you have your cake and
your paleo lifestyle, too.
  TX773.C63157 2013
  641.86--dc23
                                                                2013012649

Cover and Book design by Duckie Designs
Photography by Heather Connell

Printed and bound in China

The information in this book is for educational purposes only. It is not intended to replace the advice of a physician or medical practitioner. Please see your health care provider before beginning any new health program.

PALEO

sweets and treats

Seasonally Inspired Desserts

THAT LET YOU HAVE YOUR CAKE AND
YOUR PALEO LIFESTYLE, TOO

♥

Heather Connell

FAIR WINDS
PRESS
BEVERLY, MASSACHUSETTS

28

75

90

122

contents

INTRODUCTION

I'm Heather—a wife, a mom, and a lover of grain-free Paleo baking and cooking. But this is not how I've always cooked and baked. You see, I grew up in the South with two amazing ladies in my life, my mom and grandmother, who both loved to be in the kitchen. I remember as a child standing on a chair beside them helping them cook their latest savory meal and bake their latest delicious dessert. Our family was all about coming together around a table, sharing a meal for every holiday and celebration in our lives.

Although my grandmother and mom had a love for cooking, I never adopted this passion until I got married and realized I had to feed another person. As scary as that was, I dove in face first, which meant reading lots of cookbooks and watching many cooking shows. Along the way and after many disasters, I got better in the kitchen, and my love of cooking grew deeper. Instead of taking the route of the Southern fried foods I grew up with, however, I took a more healthy approach (or so I thought). But I still incorporated the grain- and sugar-based baking my mom and grandmother taught me. I thought this direction was the right one, but my world was about to suddenly change and I was going to be faced with an unfamiliar challenge.

A little more than a year after the birth of my twin daughters, I was experiencing stomach pains, fatigue, and many other health problems. After five or six months of monthly doctor's visits to continually monitor suspicious findings that were going on in my body, I became frustrated and tired, even more than I already was. The doctor finally said it was either go on medication to hope-fully help these "things" go away or undergo surgery. Becoming more frustrated and very scared, I decided to put an end to these "feelings" and research the "whys." I soon found out that many of my health issues were coming from my very own kitchen—all the foods I loved, the foods that I thought were right.

I began to remove culprits such as gluten, dairy, and soy from my diet and gradually started to feel better, but it wasn't until I stumbled across this new thing called Paleo that I started to feel fantastic. All those health problems that once ailed me disappeared within thirty to forty days, and it was almost like I could see more clearly. A beautiful thing when I had felt so foggy for so long! I was like a new person. And I had a second chance.

As much as I loved this new feeling I was having, my kitchen became foreign to me. The things I used to love to eat were now forbidden. In ways, it was like learning to cook all over again. Before Paleo, I loved to bake. Again, it was something my grandmother and mom taught me. It was something I planned to teach my beautiful daughters. But how do you bake in a Paleo kitchen when Paleo circles frown upon "treats"?

I've always loved a challenge. After all, everyone deserves a little indulgence from time to time— but without the guilt or health-robbing effects. I got in the kitchen and embraced my new lifestyle. The beautiful thing was that my twin daughters were by my side for this journey. We soon found ourselves creating delicious "treats" while using only seasonal whole foods with sparing amounts of natural sweeteners. Not only was I teaching myself, but I was also teaching my daughters about whole real foods and taking care of our health. We visited the local markets and picked out seasonal produce to use in our kitchen. We learned how to cook in this new way together. Such an amazing and beautiful thing! Paleo hasn't changed just my life—it has also changed my family's.

Throughout this journey, I shared everything with my readers on my blog, MultiplyDelicious.com, from the reasons behind my new lifestyle to recipes. Because of my readers and the questions I received behind the scenes in emails, I wanted to learn more so I could help others out there. I received my Holistic Nutritionist certification in hopes that I could share my knowledge and help others in their journey toward better health. I find it amazing that what we put into our bodies can really heal us. It did for me! And I promise, it's not hard.

As Paleo eaters, we can still have the foods that make our hearts smile and our stomachs dance with delight. This is why I have written this book, to help you both embrace your Paleo kitchen and reward yourself with seasonal whole treats that you and your body can feel good about.

I'm thrilled you are reading this book and hope my recipes will find a home in your kitchen. I also hope you'll discover, as I have, that eating whole foods directly from the source—our earth—with fewer chemicals and less processing, is not only perfectly doable but also perfectly delicious! And don't be surprised when your friends and family (including kids) say, "I can't believe this dessert is Paleo. It's delicious!"

♥

chapter one

PALEO: THE HOW TOS
WHAT IS "PALEO"?

The Paleo (or Paleolithic) Diet is a lifestyle based on the ancestral human diet. It resembles the eating habits of our Paleolithic ancestors (the "hunters and gatherers"), who, if they were able to avoid illness (having no modern medicine), lived very long and healthy lives.

THE BASICS OF EATING PALEO

Let's break this down so we can all understand. Simply put, Paleo is about eating the same whole foods that were found in nature millions of years ago. Now, what do I mean when I say "whole foods"? Think foods that come from the land, such as meats, vegetables, fruits, nuts, and seeds. These foods are high in fat and protein, low in carbohydrates, and free of all the ingredients we can't pronounce.

If you're anything like I was when I started down the Paleo path, you want to know what you can't or shouldn't have. The things you should avoid include processed, refined, nutrient-poor foods such as grains, soy, legumes, dairy, industrial seed oils (like corn, cottonseed, soybean, canola, or grapeseed), and artificial and processed sugars and additives. What you can have: *real* food! Let me show you what I mean.

EAT WHOLE FOODS

Meat, Seafood, and Eggs: It is ideal to enjoy meat and seafood from grass- and organic-fed, pastured-raised, or wild-caught, sustainable sources. Like us, animals and fish can't properly digest grains, so if I'm telling *you* not to eat grains, the animals you eat should also not eat grains. Choose meats and fish that have been raised eating their natural diets.

Vegetables and Fruits: There is an abundance of vegetables and fruits from season to season that I urge you to explore. You don't always have to have the same option day after day. Add variety to your day by changing up your vegetables and fruits depending on what is in season—not necessarily what's on the grocery store shelves.

Nuts and Seeds: Nuts and seeds have a lot of beneficial nutrients. They are perfect for snacking and for incorporating into Paleo baking as grain-free flour substitutes or as nut butters that can be an alternative to oils in some recipes. I do want to caution you against eating too many nuts, however. If your health goal is fat loss, I suggest keeping your nut intake to a minimum, not as a part of your daily diet.

Fats and Oils: Choosing the best-quality fats you can find is essential to improving your health from the inside out. Fats and oils should be naturally occurring and minimally processed, such as animal fat (bacon grease/tallow), coconut oil and coconut butter, olive oil, avocado oil, macadamia nut oil, and palm oil.

Drinks: Water is your best option. Herbal teas are good, too. Coffee is okay, but in moderation. Caffeine can trigger the release of unhealthy levels of the hormone cortisol in some people. Chronically elevated cortisol levels are bad news for many reasons (think weight gain, disruptive sleep patterns, and stressed immune system).

ELIMINATE REFINED FOODS

Grains: These include, but are not limited to, wheat, barley, rye, spelt, corn, rice, quinoa, millet, bulgur wheat, buckwheat, and amaranth.

Legumes: Beans, peas, lentils, and soy contain antinutrients that can rob the body of valuable minerals. Legumes are often regarded as a healthy dietary choice, based on their fiber, vitamin and mineral, and "high" protein content. However, beans are primarily a source of carbohydrates, not protein, and our bodies can't properly break them down. And sorry, folks, no peanut butter either. Peanuts contain a protein called lectin that can provoke an immune response in the stomach, promoting inflammation in the body. Opt instead for almond or cashew butter or seed butters such as sunflower.

Packaged Foods: Anything that is packaged that has a long list of stuff you don't know or can't pronounce is probably not going to be your best food choice. Basically, anything that is not real food.

Processed Foods: Fast food is the big one here. Cut it out, folks.

Dairy Products: Eliminate all processed and pasteurized dairy: milk, cheese, yogurt, cottage cheese, ice cream, and frozen yogurt. Dairy provokes an inflammatory response in the gut, which can adversely affect how you digest and absorb not just dairy products but all your food.

Sugars: Say no to refined, artificial, and added sugars. Opt instead for natural sweeteners such as raw honey, maple syrup, and fruit.

Drinks: Avoid soft drinks, fruit juice (unless it's from your juicer at home), and grain-based alcohol.

Hydrogenated or Partially Hydrogenated Oils: These include margarine, buttery spreads, canola oil, peanut oil, soybean oil, corn oil, grapeseed oil, vegetable oil, sunflower oil, safflower oil, sesame seed oil, and shortening.

PALEO AT A GLANCE	
ENJOY	AVOID
Meats	Grains
Vegetables	Legumes
Fruits	Dairy
Nuts	Processed Foods
Seeds	Alcohol
Healthy Fats	Starches

OTHER THINGS TO KEEP IN MIND

Sleep, at least seven to eight hours a night. If you can swing more, I highly recommend it.

Avoid alcohol. If you absolutely have to, wines are the "better" option to consume. Wine has a low alcohol content and is rich in heart-healthy antioxidants such as resveratrol. Plus, wines are essentially fermented fruits.

Exercise! You can change your diet, but you also need to be active. Aim for at least three to four days a week of heart-pumping movement.

YOU *CAN* HAVE YOUR CAKE AND YOUR PALEO LIFESTYLE, TOO

But in moderation. By no means am I going to tell you to indulge in sweets and treats every day. The idea behind *Paleo Sweets and Treats* is to provide you with better choices when you have to have that special treat. Life still happens when you're following a Paleo lifestyle, and my goal is for you to keep enjoying it while staying Paleo. There will still be holiday gatherings, birthdays, celebrations, and other occasions, and you can still stay on track with the recipes in this book. I provide eighty-five recipes that will keep you from giving in to the carb- and sugar-laden desserts in your grocery store aisles that you once indulged in. I will help you stay on track by providing better choices for occasional treats that are still Paleo, using nutritionally dense, seasonal produce and all natural sweeteners.

I'm a huge believer that even though you are following the Paleo lifestyle, you can still get in the kitchen with your friends and family and bake. Many of the memories I have from growing up involve baking with my mom and grandmother, laughing, learning, making messes, and just having fun. You can still create these wonderful times in your life with a Paleo baking kitchen. Trust me. I've already created amazing memories with my kids. Even better, they are learning what is truly rewarding for their bodies.

People believe eating whole foods is hard or limiting, but it isn't. I remember feeling simply overwhelmed when I started down the Paleo path. I was one of those people who thought it was going to be hard, and my first instinct was *I can't do this*. But I did, and I'm here to tell you that you can, too. It's simply a matter of making better food choices that in the end will promote better health in your body. Sure, in the beginning it will be an adjustment, but in the end it will be a lifestyle.

So get in your kitchen and create, enjoy, and have fun while staying Paleo. You'll be using high-quality Paleo ingredients and seasonal produce. The tasty Paleo treats in this book are for those special times in your life that are worth celebrating.

♥

chapter two

STOCKING YOUR PALEO BAKING PANTRY

When I made the switch to Paleo, I had to teach myself how to cook all over again, but when it came to baking, I really had to learn everything from scratch. Paleo baking is a lot different from the traditional ways of baking. With traditional baking, you become accustomed to using things such as all-purpose flour, sugar, brown sugar, and cornstarch—just to name a few of the items I used to keep in my non-Paleo kitchen. "Traditional" baking ingredients aren't nutrient dense, and they are definitely not Paleo. Throw them away and never look back.

Your next question might be, what should you have in your Paleo baking pantry? Well, with this chapter, I will guide you in the right direction for stocking your kitchen for successful Paleo baking. I've also included some insights on certain ingredients that will help you transition to Paleo baking. Let this journey be a fun one, and keep in the back of your mind that you are making changes that will reward you and those you love.

GRAIN-FREE FLOURS

You will find only four grain-free flours throughout *Paleo Sweets and Treats*. This is because I have found these to be the staple grain-free flours that work best in my Paleo baking kitchen.

COCONUT FLOUR

Coconut flour offers a gluten-free alternative to traditional grain-based flours. I've come to enjoy and prefer baking with coconut flour because it produces light and airy cupcakes and cakes. Coconut flour, which is made from grinding coconut pulp after it has been squeezed for coconut milk, produces a soft flour. It is high in fiber, protein, and fat, which makes it exceptionally filling. It's also a good source of lauric acid, a saturated fat thought to support the immune system and the thyroid. Coconut flour is a great source of manganese, which helps you better utilize many nutrients, including choline and biotin (found in eggs), vitamin C, and thiamin. Manganese also helps maintain optimal blood sugar levels.

Coconut Flour Tips

♥ **Adjust Your Ratios.** In baking with coconut flour, you cannot substitute coconut flour for wheat or other grain-based flours at a 1:1 ratio. They are not equivalent. Coconut flour is extraordinarily absorbent, and a little goes a long way.

Generally, you want to substitute ¼ cup to ⅓ cup (30 to 40 g) coconut flour for every ¾ cup to 1 cup (90 to 120 g) grain-based flour or nut flour. You will need to increase the number of eggs and liquid when using coconut flour. The general ratio rule I follow is ½ cup (60 g) coconut flour plus 5 eggs plus ½ cup (120 ml) coconut milk (or other liquid). This ratio will vary depending on the other ingredients in the recipe; for example, if the recipe calls for mashed bananas, the bananas will add extra moisture to the batter, so you'll need to reduce another liquid, say coconut milk, by ¼ cup (60 ml). And if I'm adding cacao powder to a recipe, I usually adjust the flour down a little or increase the liquid slightly because cacao powder also absorbs moisture.

♥ **Break Up Lumps.** Coconut flour tends to be clumpy, so sifting the flour before mixing it into a recipe will help you avoid finding clumps in your baked goods. I tend to place my batters in a food processor, which helps break down the clumps without having to sift the flour.

♥ **Store It Dry.** Coconut flour is best if stored at room temperature in your pantry.

ALMOND FLOUR

Almond flour is made from blanched, finely ground nuts. It is quite high in protein; rich in vitamin E, many B vitamins, manganese, potassium, calcium, iron, magnesium, zinc, and selenium; and is lower in omega-6 polyunsaturated fats per gram than many other nuts. When baking with almond flour, you can use similar quantities to regular flour in your recipe, but keep in mind that because almond flour does not contain gluten, it doesn't yield the elasticity or hold together the way wheat flour does. If a recipe calls for a different nut flour, such as hazelnut, you can substitute 1:1 with almond flour.

Almond Flour Tips

- ♥ **Pay Attention to the Grind.** The finer the almonds are ground, the better your baked goods will turn out. If you use coarser ground flour, your product will be grainy and the texture will be as if you added nuts to the batter.

- ♥ **Monitor Heat.** Nut flours burn easily, so when baking with them, keep the temperatures lower by about 25°F to 50°F (4° to 10°C) and bake for slightly longer. Keep a close eye on your baked goods, as all ovens heat differently.

- ♥ **Store It Cold.** Almond flour is best if stored in your refrigerator or freezer. It will keep for a month in the refrigerator and 6 to 8 months in the freezer. If you store it in the freezer, just remove the portion you need for your recipe and let it come to room temperature for 20 minutes.

ALMOND MEAL

Almond meal is quite simply skin-on almonds that are milled into a coarse flour. It has a fraction of the carbs of gluten flours and provides a hearty flavor and consistency without adding empty calories. Almond meal is full of protein and dietary fiber similar to that of almond flour. I prefer to use almond meal in crumbles because of the coarser texture.

HAZELNUT FLOUR OR MEAL

Hazelnut flour or meal is made from pure, ground hazelnuts. Sweeter and slightly coarser than its almond flour cousin, it is a good source of dietary fiber and protein. It's perfect for adding rich flavor to all baked goods, from muffins to cakes and cookies; use it the way you would almond flour or meal.

FATS AND OILS

When choosing fats and oils, I avoid the darlings of the health food industry—grapeseed oil, canola oil, and rice bran oil—because these oils are not traditional fats, and their processing method negates their healthfulness. Instead, I choose fats that offer true nourishment in the way of fat-soluble vitamins and naturally occurring antioxidants and that are minimally processed.

COCONUT OIL

This mildly sweet, fragrant oil is deeply resonant of the tropics. Unrefined extra-virgin coconut oil provides a beautiful flavor to baked dishes. It plays an enormous role in the traditional diets of South Pacific islanders, who enjoyed resilient health prior to the widespread availability of processed foods, sugars, and industrial vegetable oils. Coconut oil has been under much debate in years past due to its saturated fat content, but this medium-chain fatty acid has since been redeemed because of its health benefits. It is rich in lauric acid (a fat that has high antimicrobial properties), is quickly used for energy, and contributes to the health of the immune system. Coconut oil is also rapidly converted into energy in the liver, and it increases metabolic rate.

Coconut Oil Tips

♥ **Purer Is Better.** Seek out unrefined, virgin-pressed coconut oil in a dark bottle or heavy-duty glass or plastic container.

♥ **Use Equal Ratios.** Use coconut oil at a 1:1 ratio to replace vegetable oils, margarine, shortening, and/or butter in baking.

♥ **Mind the Smoke Point.** Coconut oil is a very stable oil even at higher temperatures. However, it is best not to cook beyond the smoke point (450°F [230°C, or gas mark 8]) of coconut oil, because it will begin to deteriorate the oil and turn it yellow. This is mostly a concern when cooking with the oil, as opposed to baking with it, but it's important to know.

♥ **Do Not Refrigerate.** Keep coconut oil in a cool, dark cupboard. Refrigeration makes the oil hard and difficult to measure. Most recipes in this book call for melting the coconut oil in order to incorporate it into the recipes, but you first have to measure the amount the recipe calls for in solid form and then melt it.

COCONUT BUTTER

Coconut butter is freshly made from whole coconut flesh (not just the oil) and puréed into a fibrous, densely nutritious spread. Coconut oil separation may occur, causing a white, solid top layer on the coconut butter. Simply warm and blend together. Also, refrigeration is not recommended with coconut butter.

GRASS-FED BUTTER, CLARIFIED BUTTER, AND GHEE

Butter offers a soft flavor—sweet and comforting—and it brings an old-fashioned creaminess to recipes. Like most highly saturated fats, butter has gotten a bad rap as industrial oils have usurped its rightful place at the kitchen table. But grass-fed butter that's free of industrial feed and hormones provides deep nourishment. When produced from the cream of grass-fed cows, butter is extraordinarily rich in fat-soluble vitamins A, D, E, and K_2. Further, it is a rich source of the antioxidant beta-carotene, which accounts for its lush golden color.

Clarified butter and ghee come from butter, but both have been slowly melted and then filtered to remove their milk solids. The resultant fat is free from offending proteins and sugars and is often well tolerated by those suffering from dairy sensitivities.

Grass-Fed Butter, Clarified Butter, and Ghee Tips

♥ **Mind the Smoke Point.** Butter has a low smoke point of about 350°F (180°C, or gas mark 4) and is therefore suitable for low-temperature cooking and baking. Clarified butter and ghee can tolerate higher heats, up to 485°F (252°C, or gas mark 9), due to the removal of milk solids.

NATURAL SWEETENERS

As with all foods, the sweeteners you choose should be whole and unrefined: raw honey, maple syrup, and molasses are all good options for natural sweeteners. You should avoid agave nectar, raw agave nectar, corn syrup, and white and brown sugars, as well as liquid and powdered stevia, xylitol, and sugar alcohols, because they are all heavily processed. And those pink and yellow packets on most tables of restaurants? Avoid those, too.

RAW HONEY

This wonderfully rich golden liquid is the product of honey bees and a naturally delicious alternative to white sugar. Although it is available throughout the year, it is an exceptional treat in the summer and fall, when it has just been harvested and is at its freshest. Not all honey is created equally. Raw organic honey tends to have higher health benefits due to its antibacterial, antiviral, and antifungal qualities. This is the reason raw honey is my choice when baking, and the one I recommend any time honey is called for in a recipe.

PURE MAPLE SYRUP

Maple syrup is one of the many wonders of the world. This amber liquid with its earthy sweet taste is made from the sap of the sugar, black, or red maple tree. Maple syrup contains fewer calories and a higher concentration of minerals than honey does. When baking, I prefer to use pure Grade B maple syrup, as opposed to Grade A, because of its great flavor and high level of sweetness, which means you can use less and still achieve the flavor you are looking for. Another benefit is maple syrup doesn't break down during the baking process the way artificial sweeteners do.

MOLASSES

Unsulfured molasses has a syrup consistency to it and provides the robust bittersweet flavor we love in gingerbread. And even better, molasses is a sweetener that is actually good for you. Unlike refined white sugar and corn syrup, which are stripped of virtually all nutrients except simple carbohydrates, or artificial sweeteners like saccharin or aspartame, which not only provide no useful nutrients but also have been shown to cause health problems, molasses is a sweetener that contains significant amounts of a variety of minerals that promote health: iron, calcium, cooper, manganese, potassium, and magnesium.

DATES

Dates are a fruit that are sweet in taste and rich in minerals and vitamins such as B_1, B_2, B_3, and B_5 along with A and C, and is high in iron and potassium. In fact, ounce for ounce, dates have more potassium than a banana.

Fresh Medjool dates can add a natural form of sweetness to a dessert. You will be surprised by how a few dates go a long way to create dishes similar to the sweetness of your pre-Paleo desserts, but without the guilt.

Date Tips

♥ **Mash Them Up.** If your dates are not soft or are a little dry, add enough boiling water to just cover them and allow them to sit for a few minutes. Then drain all but a tablespoon (15 ml) of the water and mash the dates with a fork. The hot water will add the moisture you need to bring them to a puréed form for a recipe.

♥ **Keep the Pits.** Remember to purchase pit-in dates, because they contain more moisture than their pitted counterparts. Before using, simply remove the interior pit by cutting the date in half.

♥ **Keep Them Fresh.** When searching the aisles of your local health food store, look first in the produce section for your dates. This is where you will find the freshest options. For optimal use, store dates in the manner they were stored when you purchased them.

FRESH HERBS AND SPICES

Fresh herbs and spices bring life to dishes. They are regarded as the first real "functional foods" because they have been grown and cultivated for thousands of years and have a long history of medicinal use. Modern-day researchers are beginning to prove that these culinary treasures can help consumers eat healthier diets by adding flavor without calories, fat, or sugar and by providing healthy phytonutrient-rich antioxidants. Here are a few that I always keep stocked in my baking kitchen.

FRESH HERBS AND SPICES		
Allspice	Cardamom	Ground cinnamon and cinnamon sticks
Ground nutmeg	Ground and whole cloves	Fresh and ground ginger
Fresh and ground ginger	Fresh basil	Fresh mint
Pumpkin pie spice	Vanilla bean and extract	

NUTS, SEEDS, AND DRIED FRUITS

Nuts and seeds are rich in proteins, healthy fats, and enzymes. All nuts, as well as the butters that are made from them, are good to include in your Paleo baking. Remember, *peanuts are not nuts*; they are legumes, and are not on the list of Paleo food choices. As I mentioned in the previous chapter, nuts should be used in moderation. They can be difficult for some people to digest due to their being high in digestive-enzyme inhibitors. You'll see several recipes in this book that require soaking the nuts, which helps neutralize these enzyme inhibitors.

Dried fruits are great for naturally sweetening baked goods. I use them in a couple recipes in this book, but I do recommend eating them in moderation.

NUTS, SEEDS, AND DRIED FRUITS		
Almond butter	Almonds	Cashews
Cashew butter	Hazelnuts	Pecans
Pistachios	Walnuts	Pumpkin seeds
Coconut, butter	Coconut, unsweetened shredded or flaked	Dates
Dried apricots	Dried blueberries	Dried cherries
Dried cranberries		

VEGETABLES AND FRUITS

You will find a variety of fruits and even vegetables throughout this book. I'm a huge fan of seasonal produce because of the bright colors they provide to a dish, but more important, they provide amazing flavors. When fruits and vegetables are used according to their season (refer to "Baking Seasonally," page 23), they can really make a dish—or in this case, a dessert—shine. I do want to point out that certain crops on the below list tend to absorb more pesticides than others, so I recommend purchasing those with an asterisk (*) organic whenever possible.

VEGETABLES AND FRUITS		
Acorn squash	Avocados	Butternut squash
Carrots	Sweet potatoes	Zucchini
Apples*	Apricots*	Bananas
Blackberries*	Blueberries*	Cherries*
Cranberries	Grapefruit	Kiwis
Lemons	Limes	Mangoes
Melons	Nectarines*	Oranges
Peaches*	Pears*	Pineapples
Pomegranates	Pumpkins	Raspberries*
Rhubarb	Strawberries*	Tangerines

OTHER ESSENTIALS

What follows are some other essentials that I keep on hand in my Paleo pantry; they don't fall into any exact list as the previous ingredients do. If you keep the following ingredients as well as those in the herb and spice section on hand, you'll be able to jump into many of the recipes in this book without a special trip to the grocery store. I recommend buying small quantities and replacing them often.

PASTURED FREE-RANGE EGGS

I buy eggs from local farmers with chickens that are free range and allowed to eat and live the way they are meant to live. The eggs come in a variety of colors and sizes, and they have amazing deep-orange yolks. They are delicious! It is my dream to one day have enough land to raise my own chickens, but until that day becomes a reality, I will keep getting them from the local farmer because they truly are nothing like those at the supermarket.

COCONUT MILK

Coconut milk is produced by combining the flesh of coconuts with water. It is great to bake with as an alternative to regular dairy. In my recipes, I use canned, full-fat, unsweetened coconut milk. As it sits, the fat and water separate, so before opening a can be sure to shake it to bring it back together. But in some of the recipes in this book you'll see that I ask you not to shake the can before opening because the solid part on the top can actually resemble heavy cream and can be used to make a delicious coconut whipped cream.

CHOCOLATE (CACAO POWDER, CACAO NIBS, DARK CHOCOLATE)

All the recipes involving chocolate in this book use pure cacao powder or pure baking dark chocolate, both unsweetened. I suggest always buying 100 percent cacao, which is unsweetened. Anything less than 100 percent has sugar added, and sugar is not Paleo. I prefer to buy unsweetened dark chocolate so I can sweeten it using a Paleo-friendly sweetener. If you can't get your hands on 100 percent dark chocolate, try to use a dark chocolate that is 85 percent or higher, without soy lecithin or other additives. If you can't get your hands on unsweetened pure dark chocolate in bar form, you can substitute it using cacao powder: for every ounce (28 g) of unsweetened dark chocolate, use 3 tablespoons (24 g) pure cacao powder plus 1 tablespoon (15 ml) melted coconut oil and stir to combine.

BAKING SODA AND BAKING POWDER

Baking soda is the only Paleo-friendly leavener to help you get great results in your baked goods. It loses its potency over time and should certainly be replaced every 2 to 3 months. Baking powders on the market have traces of gluten in them. There is only one recipe in this book where I suggest baking powder, and I only recommend it if you are using a grain-free and aluminum-free product made in your own kitchen. To make your own use 1 part baking soda plus 1 part cream of tartar plus 2 parts arrowroot. I usually make and store it in a leftover glass spice jar.

FINE SEA SALT

This is my everyday salt in both cooking and baking. I prefer to use Celtic sea salt, which is harvested by hand from a coastal region in France. It is minimally processed and very high in minerals. I like how it evenly distributes in baking recipes.

UNFLAVORED GELATIN

Gelatin is a colorless, flavorless thickening agent that helps give body to certain desserts. Gelatin must be softened before using. All of the recipes using gelatin in *Paleo Sweets and Treats* will walk you through this step, but commonly for every 1 tablespoon (17 g) of gelatin you must use ¼ cup (60 ml) liquid to dissolve it. Look in the Resources section (pages 168–169) for the brand I prefer to use.

BAKING SEASONALLY

What is seasonal eating and, by extension, baking? Quite simply, to eat seasonally means to consume fruits and vegetables only during the time of year, or season, in which they are harvested. Our ancestors ate seasonal food because they didn't have much of a choice. They didn't have the option of going to the local supermarket and buying strawberries in January or asparagus trucked in from across the country. Living off the land ensured that what they were eating was fresh and nutrient dense—and of course it was unadulterated by pesticides, chemicals, or crop modification. We, on the other hand, need to make a conscious and educated choice in selecting only those foods that are grown seasonally and locally. Why, you may ask? Here are some of the benefits that you'll achieve by choosing only seasonal produce next time you are at your local market.

It's more nutritious. As soon as a fruit or vegetable is harvested, nutritional breakdown occurs. Many vitamins present in fruits or vegetables before harvesting are highly unstable and are largely depleted a few days after harvest. Out-of-season produce is usually shipped many miles before reaching your local market. The more miles and days it is in transit, the more it loses its nutritional value. Buying produce at its height of seasonality means you will be getting foods that have much higher antioxidant content than nonseasonal foods and they will have an overall better nutritional content. They will also be fresher and better tasting.

It's less expensive. Buying things out of season means long shipping times, fuel costs, and other factors that all add up to a higher price tag in the end. Even if fruits and vegetables aren't shipped a great distance, growing out-of-season produce in a greenhouse still adds up to more energy (costs), which is passed on to you, the consumer. Eating seasonally means buying things that can be grown locally (or relatively locally), in their natural surroundings, weather, and climate conditions. Less energy and less transit time mean cheaper price tags in the end.

It's better for the environment. By eating seasonally and locally, you also help protect the environment by not consuming foods that take large amounts of fuel and energy to be shipped across the country. In buying local, you are helping your local farmers and supporting your local economy. Eating seasonally may not always be convenient, but if you can find local food providers in your area you will be doing a world of good for yourself, your family, your local economy, and the environment.

HOW TO SHOP IN SEASON

What's in season depends on where you live. Growing seasons vary. For example, the produce will be different in Miami from what is grown in Kansas at the same time of the year. Seek out your local farmers' markets to learn about produce seasonality for your area. I have learned a lot from my local farmer purchases. I've learned when and where these items grow near me, and that has informed how I cook and what I serve my family. Learning the seasonal growing patterns in your area will be a great value. You'll get the freshest, most nutritious food and help your community and the environment. There are resources on the Web that will guide you on what is fresh and in season for your specific state and region. See the Resources in the back of the book (pages 168–169).

Here is a quick rundown of some of the most commonly available seasonal fruits and veggies throughout the United States (international seasonal foods will vary from these). These are the foods I focus on in this book. You will see that some produce will overlap some seasons, too.

Spring

Spring is the season the earth wakes from the cold winter, as warmer temperatures start to prevail. The freshness and newness translate to the local farmers' markets and to your table. Bright greens dominate the color spectrum, but you will also see the sweetness of spring fruits such as strawberries, rhubarb, and apricots. There is nothing like going to a local strawberry patch and picking your very own bunch of sweetness.

COMMON SPRING PRODUCE

Apricots	Arugula	Asparagus	Beets
Blueberries	Carrots	Grapefruit	Kumquats
Lemons	Limes	Mangoes	Mint
Oranges	Parsley	Raspberries	Rhubarb
Spinach	Strawberries	Sweet potatoes	Tangerines

Summer

As the temperatures rise and school days end, the fun times of summer begin. Summer has amazing produce and is the season of some of my favorite fruits. Many of the fruits on this list bring back fond memories of my childhood, like sitting at my grandmother's kitchen table eating fresh cantaloupe. Or having huge slices of watermelon after playing in the heat for hours. It's amazing how fresh seasonal food can make imprints in your life.

COMMON SUMMER PRODUCE

Basil	Blackberries	Blueberries	Boysenberries
Cantaloupe	Carrots	Cherries	Figs
Grapes	Limes	Mangoes	Melons
Nectarines	Peaches	Pineapple	Plums
Raspberries	Strawberries	Summer squash	Watermelon
Zucchini			

Autumn

Cooler days after the summer heat, beautiful foliage on the trees (and ground), back-to-school routines, and holiday seasons—all are signs of the autumn months. In autumn, Nature gives us an abundance of produce in a rainbow of colors, from the orange of pumpkins and deep reds of apples to the garnets of root vegetables. For all these reasons, autumn is one of my favorite seasons to bake in. The warmth of the kitchen with the warmth of the autumn produce make the cooler temperatures outside welcoming.

COMMON AUTUMN PRODUCE			
Acorn squash	Apples	Butternut Squash	Carrots
Cranberries	Dates	Figs	Ginger
Grapes	Pears	Pecans	Plums
Pomegranates	Pumpkin	Rutabaga	Sweet potatoes

Winter

Winter brings cooler temperatures and makes us crave things that warm our soul. Winter does supply less produce than other seasons, but it is packed with great citrus flavors that can transport you to warmer temperatures. If you live in a climate where citrus fruits aren't your local crop, then opt for those that travel the shortest distance to where you are.

COMMON WINTER PRODUCE			
Clementines	Cranberries	Dates	Grapefruit
Kiwi	Kumquats	Lemons	Limes
Mandarins	Oranges	Pears	Persimmons
Pomegranate	Red currants	Rutabaga	Sweet potatoes
Tangerines			

In the next chapters, I will share my recipes for treats that use fresh seasonal produce. With these recipes you will discover the pleasures of eating seasonally—without sugar, without grains, and without processed, unnatural ingredients—all in three simple steps: shop for what's fresh; cook with inspiration from the pages of this book; and eat the delicious Paleo results.

chapter three

♥

SPRING'S BLESSING:
FRESH FLAVORS TO WAKE UP THE TASTE BUDS

Spring brings fresh beginnings as the days grow progressively warmer and shine with increased beautiful sunlight. Those winter comfort desserts are replaced with light and refreshing desserts. Spring starts with lemon, the sunnier, tart citrus fruit that carries over from the winter. Rhubarb marks the true beginning of spring. Then enter the ruby-red strawberries, the queen of spring-time fruits. Apricots, those beautifully orange colored darlings, arrive just before the start of summer. All of these favorite fruits of spring make this season's desserts refreshing and tasty.

- **Lemons:** Lemons more commonly evoke images of sunshine and summer as homemade lemonade stands can attest. These oval yellow fruits are powerhouses when you want to bring out the flavor of other foods, like the berries in the Lemon Berry Custard Pie (page 38). But don't be fooled, because they can pack a punch of flavor on their own, too.

- **Rhubarb:** Tart and sweet in flavor, this vegetable-that's-used-like-a-fruit looks like red celery, but don't let its stalks scare you away. They are actually rich in several B-complex vitamins. Rhubarb is also an excellent source of vitamin C and is high in dietary fiber. It's readily available from April through June or July. Enjoy the Honey Mint Rhubarb Sorbet (page 35) on a hot summer day.

- **Strawberries:** The fragrantly sweet juiciness and deep red color of strawberries can brighten up both the taste and the aesthetics of a dish. They are among the fruits (and vegetables) ranked highest in health-promoting antioxidants. Although they have become increasingly available year-round, they are at the peak of their season from April through July, when they are the most delicious and most abundant. A favorite way to use fresh strawberries is in the Strawberry Short-cake Cupcakes (page 32).

- **Apricots:** Apricots are those beautiful orange fuzzy-soft fruits full of beta-carotene and fiber that are one of the first signs that spring is coming to an end and summer is around the corner. Although dried apricots are available year-round, fresh apricots with a plentiful supply of vitamin C are in season from the end of April through August. If you're looking for a great way to use your fresh ripened apricots, the Apricot Crumb Cake (page 47) is perfect.

Lemon Bars

These tangy, tart lemon bars have a smooth and creamy filling nestled up against a coconut-spiked crust. They are the perfect refreshing springtime dessert for when the temperatures start to warm up. A nutritional tidbit about lemons: They help strengthen the immune system and aid in fighting disease.

FOR CRUST:

2 eggs

¼ cup (55 g) extra-virgin unrefined coconut oil, melted

3 tablespoons (60 g) raw honey

½ cup (60 g) coconut flour

¾ cup (60 g) unsweetened shredded coconut, divided

¼ teaspoon ground cinnamon

¼ teaspoon baking soda

Pinch of sea salt

FOR FILLING:

1 cup (235 ml) fresh lemon juice (from 5 to 6 lemons)

2 teaspoons (2.5 g) lemon zest

6 eggs

2 tablespoons (40 g) raw honey

2 tablespoons (30 ml) maple syrup

⅛ teaspoon sea salt

½ cup (109 g) extra-virgin unrefined coconut oil, melted

1 teaspoon (5 ml) vanilla extract

½ cup (40 g) unsweetened shredded coconut

Preheat the oven to 350°F (180°C, or gas mark 4). Line an 8 x 8-inch (20 x 20 cm) glass baking dish with parchment paper, allowing the paper to go up the edges of the dish.

To make the crust: In the bowl of a food processor, combine the eggs, coconut oil, and honey and process until smooth. Add the coconut flour, ¼ cup (20 g) of the shredded coconut, cinnamon, baking soda, and salt and process again until well combined.

Remove the blade from the bowl and stir in the remaining ½ cup (40 g) shredded coconut. Press the crust evenly into the prepared baking dish and bake for 15 to 18 minutes, or until the edges are just turning golden. Allow the crust to cool.

To make the filling: In a medium saucepan over medium heat, whisk together the lemon juice, lemon zest, eggs, honey, maple syrup, and sea salt. Slowly add the melted coconut oil while whisking constantly. Whisk until it starts to thicken—it should be thick enough to coat the back of a wooden spoon. You don't want to leave this unattended. Strain the filling through a fine-mesh strainer to remove any cooked egg bits. Stir in the vanilla extract.

Pour the filling over the baked crust and sprinkle the top with the shredded coconut. Cover and refrigerate for at least 4 hours, or best overnight, to allow the curd to set.

Remove the bars from the baking dish by lifting up on the parchment paper, cut into sixteen 2 x 2-inch (5 x 5 cm) bars, and serve.

Will keep in the refrigerator for up to 4 days.

MAKES 16 BARS

Lemon-Coconut Tarts

These yummy tarts require no baking and are a great refreshing treat. Want to change it up? Switch out the lemon for a lime and you have a key lime-like tart.

FOR CRUST:

1½ cups (180 g) almond flour

⅓ cup (27 g) unsweetened shredded coconut

3 tablespoons (41 ml) extra-virgin unrefined coconut oil, melted

1½ tablespoons (30 g) raw honey

¼ teaspoon sea salt

¼ teaspoon ground cinnamon

1 Medjool date, pitted and chopped

FOR FILLING:

1½ cups (200 g) raw cashews, soaked in water overnight at room temperature

2 tablespoons (27 ml) extra-virgin unrefined coconut oil, melted

2 tablespoons (30 ml) fresh lemon juice

1 tablespoon (15 ml) canned coconut milk

2 tablespoons (40 g) raw honey

1 teaspoon (5 ml) vanilla extract

1 teaspoon (1.7 g) lemon zest

2 tablespoons (10 g) unsweetened shredded coconut, slightly toasted

To make the crust: Place the almond flour, shredded coconut, coconut oil, honey, salt, cinnamon, and date in the bowl of a food processor or blender and process until smooth. Divide the crust mixture into 4 portions and press each portion into the bottom and up the sides of four 3-inch (7.5 cm) tart pans. Chill the crusts in the tart pans in the refrigerator while you make the filling.

To make the filling: Drain the cashews and place them in the bowl of a food processor with the coconut oil, lemon juice, coconut milk, honey, vanilla extract, and lemon zest and process until smooth, 2 to 3 minutes. Divide the mixture evenly among the 4 tart crusts and sprinkle with the toasted coconut. Chill overnight. Best served cold.

Tarts keep, covered, in the refrigerator for up to 4 days.

MAKES FOUR 3-INCH (7.5 CM) TARTS

Note: Preheat oven to 325°F (170°C, or gas mark 2). Spread coconut flakes on a baking sheet in a thin layer and bake in preheated oven. The flakes will toast very quickly and won't take more than 5 to 10 minutes. After a few minutes, stir the coconut to help ensure even color.

Strawberry Shortcake Cupcakes

The fresh strawberries in both the cake and the frosting make each bite of these cupcakes strawberry bliss.

FOR CUPCAKES:

7 eggs

4 Medjool dates, pitted

½ cup (120 ml) canned coconut milk

5 tablespoons (68 g) extra-virgin unrefined coconut oil, melted

2 tablespoons (40 g) raw honey

2 teaspoons (30 ml) vanilla extract

¾ cup (90 g) coconut flour

1 teaspoon (4.6 g) baking soda

½ teaspoon sea salt

½ cup (85 g) finely chopped fresh strawberries

FOR WHIPPED CREAM:

2 cans (13½ ounces, or 400 ml each) coconut milk, refrigerated overnight

1 tablespoon (20 g) raw honey

½ teaspoon vanilla extract

¼ cup (42 g) sliced fresh strawberries

Preheat the oven to 350°F (180°C, or gas mark 4). Line a 12-cup muffin pan with paper liners, and set aside.

To make the cupcakes: In the bowl of a food processor, add the eggs, dates, coconut milk, coconut oil, honey, and vanilla and process until smooth and the dates are broken up.

In a small bowl, whisk together the coconut flour, baking soda, and salt. Add the dry ingredients to the bowl of the food processor and process until the mixture is well combined. Remove the blade from the food processor and stir in the chopped strawberries.

Divide the batter evenly among the prepared muffin cups. Bake for 30 to 35 minutes, or until golden and a toothpick inserted into the center comes out clean.

Allow the cupcakes to cool completely.

To make the cream: Carefully open the cans of coconut milk without shaking or turning them upside down. Remove the layer of coconut cream that has settled at the top of the can. Place the coconut cream in a bowl with the honey and vanilla. Using a hand mixer, mix until the cream starts to form soft peaks.

Using a pastry bag, pipe the cream onto the cooled cupcakes, or use a butter knife to spread on the cupcakes. Garnish the tops of the cupcakes with the sliced strawberries.

Cupcakes can be stored in an airtight container in the refrigerator up to 2 days.

MAKES 12 CUPCAKES

Lemon Cookies

These zesty lemon cookies are the perfect addition to a springtime baby shower or wedding shower, using a cookie cutter fitted for the occasion.

1¾ cups (210 g) almond flour

½ teaspoon baking soda

½ teaspoon unflavored gelatin

¼ teaspoon ground ginger

¼ teaspoon sea salt

2 tablespoons (27 g) extra-virgin unrefined coconut oil, melted

2 tablespoons (40 g) raw honey

1 tablespoon (15 ml) canned coconut milk

1 teaspoon (5 ml) vanilla extract

1½ teaspoons (2.5 g) lemon zest

Preheat the oven to 350°F (180°C, or gas mark 4). Line a baking sheet with parchment paper and set aside.

In a small bowl, whisk together the almond flour, baking soda, gelatin, ginger, and sea salt.

In a large bowl, combine the coconut oil, honey, coconut milk, vanilla, and lemon zest. Stir the dry ingredients into the wet, and mix until well incorporated. Form the dough into a ball, wrap with plastic wrap, and chill for 20 to 30 minutes.

Place the dough on a piece of parchment paper that has been dusted with coconut flour. Dust the top of the dough with additional coconut flour and place another piece of parchment paper, in equal size to the bottom piece, on top. Roll out the dough between the parchment papers until ¼-inch (6 mm) thick. Cut out cookies with your cookie cutter of choice and carefully place on the prepared baking sheet. Roll out the remaining dough again to cut out additional cookies.

Bake the cookies for 8 to 10 minutes, or until just golden around the edges.

Allow the cookies to cool for 5 to 10 minutes on the pan before transferring them to a wire rack to cool completely.

Cookies can be stored in an airtight container in a cool, dry place for up to 4 days. Cookies can also be frozen for up to 2 weeks.

MAKES 12 TO 18 COOKIES, DEPENDING ON COOKIE CUTTER

Honey Mint Rhubarb Sorbet

Rhubarb is typically used in sauces, jams, or pies, but I happen to like it made into a refreshing sorbet. The added honey, mint, and ginger complement the rhubarb's tang in this sorbet.

3 cups (300 g) chopped rhubarb

1 cup (235 ml) water

½ cup (160 g) raw honey

1 teaspoon (2 g) minced fresh ginger

2 tablespoons (30 ml) fresh lemon juice

2 or 3 mint leaves

¼ teaspoon sea salt

In a nonreactive medium saucepan over medium heat, combine the rhubarb, water, honey, ginger, lemon juice, mint leaves, and salt. Bring to a low simmer and cook until the rhubarb is completely soft, 10 to 15 minutes. Remove the mint leaves and transfer the rhubarb mixture to a food processor or blender. Process until the mixture is puréed.

Chill the purée in an airtight container in the refrigerator for 4 hours or overnight.

Remove the rhubarb mixture from the refrigerator and place into the bowl of an ice cream maker. Following the instructions of the machine, make sorbet (usually takes 25 to 30 minutes).

This is best enjoyed right away, but it can be stored in the freezer up to 3 weeks and enjoyed later.

MAKES ABOUT 1 PINT (285 G)

Baked Coconut Custard with Fresh Berry–Mint Compote

All you need to elevate fresh berries to dessert status is some creamy custard enriched with vanilla, honey, and fresh mint.

FOR COCONUT CUSTARD:

1 can (13½ ounces, or 400 ml) coconut milk

2 cinnamon sticks

5 whole cloves

3 egg yolks

¼ cup (80 g) raw honey

1 teaspoon (5 ml) vanilla extract

FOR COMPOTE:

½ cup (85 g) roughly chopped strawberries

¼ cup (32 g) fresh raspberries

1 teaspoon (5 ml) lemon juice

1 sprig fresh mint, leaves finely chopped

Preheat the oven to 400°F (200°C, or gas mark 6). Lightly grease four 6-ounce (168 g) or six 4-ounce (112 g) oven-safe glass jars or ramekins with coconut oil. Bring a kettle of water to a boil.

To make the custard: In a medium saucepan over medium heat, combine the coconut milk, cinnamon sticks, and cloves.

While the coconut milk is heating, whisk together the egg yolks, honey, and vanilla until smooth. When the coconut milk mixture is hot but not boiling, slowly pour it into the egg mixture while whisking. Mix well.

Pour the mixture into a sieve over a bowl and discard the cinnamon sticks and cloves. Pour the custard mixture into the jars or ramekins. Transfer the jars to a roasting pan or an ovenproof casserole dish and fill the pan with just enough boiling water to come halfway up the sides of the jars. Bake until set, 20 to 25 minutes, depending on size. Remove from the oven and water bath and set aside until cooled to room temperature.

To make the compote: In a small nonreactive bowl (such as glass), combine the berries, lemon juice, and mint. Top each custard with the berry mixture. Cover and refrigerate until set. Make up to 1 day in advance.

Custards should be covered, stored in the refrigerator, and enjoyed within 2 days.

MAKES 4 OR 6 CUSTARDS

Lemon Berry Custard Pie

This dessert is my go-to dessert in late spring and even into early summer, when the berries are at their freshest and are in abundance at the local market. Have fun with decorating the top of this pie, too. My kids and I always have fun decorating this pie together. You may be surprised what you can create with just berries.

FOR CRUST:

2 cups (240 g) almond flour

¼ cup (30 g) coconut flour

½ teaspoon unflavored gelatin

¼ teaspoon sea salt

2 Medjool dates, pitted

⅓ cup (73 g) extra-virgin unrefined coconut oil, melted

1 tablespoon (20 g) raw honey

FOR CUSTARD FILLING:

3 egg yolks

¼ cup (80 g) raw honey

1 teaspoon (5 ml) vanilla extract

1 cup (235 ml) canned coconut milk

1½ teaspoons (3.5 g) unflavored gelatin

1 tablespoon (15 ml) lemon juice

½ teaspoon lemon zest

1 cup (225 g) coconut cream (see Note, page 39)

2½ cups (363 g) fresh seasonal berries (strawberries, blueberries, or raspberries)

To make the crust: Place the almond flour, coconut flour, gelatin, and salt in the bowl of a food processor and pulse to combine. Add the dates, coconut oil, and honey and process again until a dough forms. Press the dough onto the bottom and up the sides of a 9-inch (23 cm) pie plate or pan. Chill the crust in the refrigerator for 30 minutes.

Preheat the oven to 350°F (180°C, or gas mark 4).

Remove the crust from the refrigerator and bake for 15 minutes, or until the crust is lightly golden. Transfer the crust to a wire rack and cool completely.

To make the custard filling: Whisk together the egg yolks, honey, and vanilla in a bowl.

In a small saucepan heat the coconut milk over medium-high heat for 2 to 3 minutes. Slowly pour the heated coconut milk into the egg yolk mixture, whisking constantly. Return the mixture to the saucepan and heat for an additional 2 to 3 minutes while constantly whisking. Add the gelatin and lemon juice and whisk until dissolved. Continue heating the mixture for 4 to 5 minutes, or until the mixture forms a custardlike consistency and coats the back of a wooden spoon.

Pour the custard into a sieve over a bowl to remove any egg bits. Stir in the lemon zest. Cover the bowl with plastic wrap and place in the refrigerator for at least 4 hours, or overnight.

Remove the custard from the refrigerator and add the coconut cream. Mix together using a hand mixer until the custard becomes thick and creamy.

Spread the mixture into the cooled pie crust and cover and refrigerate for 30 minutes to 1 hour to allow the custard to set. Remove from the refrigerator and arrange the berries on the top of the pie.

Refrigerate the pie until ready to serve. Then slice and enjoy.

Pie is best covered, stored in the refrigerator, and enjoyed within 2 days.

MAKES ONE 9-INCH (23 CM) PIE

Strawberry-Lemon Fruit Dip with Fruit Kebabs

I served these kebabs at a playdate my kids had with their friends one afternoon, and they were a huge hit. There is something about the simple act of poking fruit onto a stick that makes these so fun. Any fruit is a good option for skewers, although fresh seasonal choices will offer the most flavor and nutrients.

1 cup (170 g) chopped fresh strawberries

¼ cup (80 g) raw honey, divided

1½ teaspoons (2.5 g) lemon zest

Pinch of sea salt

1 teaspoon (2.3 g) unflavored gelatin

3 tablespoons (45 ml) water, divided

1 tablespoon (15 ml) lemon juice

2 large egg whites

1 cup (225 g) coconut cream (see Note)

1 teaspoon (5 ml) vanilla extract

1 pint (290 g) whole strawberries

1 mango, cubed

2 bananas, cut into ½-inch (1.3 cm) pieces

Combine the chopped strawberries, 1 tablespoon (20 g) of the honey, lemon zest, and salt and let sit for 10 minutes in a blender. Then blend until smooth.

In a large bowl, sprinkle the gelatin over 2 tablespoons (30 ml) of the water and let stand for 5 minutes.

Meanwhile, in a small saucepan over medium heat, combine the remaining 3 tablespoons (60 g) honey, lemon juice, and remaining 1 tablespoon (15 ml) water. Bring to a simmer and cook for 4 minutes.

Add the egg whites to the gelatin mixture and whip with a hand mixer until foamy, about 1 minute. Slowly pour into the hot honey mixture, whipping to form peaks.

In a separate bowl, whip the coconut cream and vanilla until soft peaks form. Fold the egg white mixture into the whipped coconut cream. Then add the strawberry mixture and gently stir to combine. Cover and chill for 2 hours, or until set.

Right before you are ready to serve, prepare fruit kebabs by alternating the whole strawberries, cubed mango, and sliced banana on 10 to 12 short wooden skewers.

The dip can be stored in an airtight container in the refrigerator for up to 4 days.

MAKES 1½ CUPS (370 G) FRUIT DIP AND 10 TO 12 SKEWERS

Note: To make the coconut cream, refrigerate 1 can (13½ ounces, or 400 ml) coconut milk overnight. Carefully open the can without shaking. Scoop the coconut cream off the top to use in this recipe.

Mango-Coconut Sherbet

We lived in South Florida for a while, and in late spring the nearby mango trees would be in plenty. Our neighbors would drop off bags every other week, and we'd eat mango-inspired dishes for days at a time. One of my kids' favorites was this light and refreshing sherbet.

2 cups (350 g) cubed peeled ripe mango

½ cup (160 g) raw honey

1 tablespoon (15 ml) fresh lime juice

1 can (13½ ounces, or 400 g) coconut milk

¼ cup (20 g) unsweetened flaked coconut, toasted (see Note, page 31)

Combine the mango, honey, lime juice, and coconut milk in a blender or food processor. Process until the mixture is smooth, scraping down the sides as necessary. Pour the mixture into the freezer can of an ice-cream maker, and freeze according to the manufacturer's instructions to soft-serve consistency. Spoon the sherbet into a freezer-safe container; cover and freeze for 2 hours, or until firm.

Sprinkle each serving of sherbet with the toasted coconut flakes.

Sherbet is best kept in the freezer for up to 3 weeks. Allow to sit for 5 minutes at room temperature, to soften, before scooping and serving.

MAKES 1 PINT (285 G)

Strawberry Banana Coconut Ice Pops

These fruit-sweetened refreshing frozen pops are perfect as the temperatures begin to rise. You can have fun with these and change the fruit up depending on what you have on hand or what is in season.

1 pound (454 g) strawberries

2 bananas

1 cup (235 ml) canned coconut milk

Toasted coconut flakes, for garnish (see Note, page 31)

Pulse the strawberries, bananas, and coconut milk together in a blender until smooth.

Divide the mixture among 6 paper cups or ice-pop molds and freeze for 1 hour. Remove from the freezer, insert wooden sticks, and sprinkle the tops with the toasted coconut flakes. Freeze until frozen, 3 to 4 hours. Best if stored in freezer up to 3 weeks.

MAKES 6 ICE POPS

Dark Chocolate Fruit Bites

These are a favorite treat of my five-year-old twin daughters. We made them last year for Valentine's Day using a small heart-shaped cookie cutter, a great alternative to the packaged chocolates their friends handed out at school.

1 banana, sliced ¼- to ½-inch (6 mm to 1.3 cm) thick

5 or 6 strawberries, stemmed and cut in half

1 or 2 kiwi, each cut crosswise into 4 slices

3 ounces (84 g) dark chocolate (85% cacao or higher)

Using a small (½-inch, or 1.3 cm) cookie cutter, cut shapes out of the banana slices. Using the cookie cutter, cut shapes out of the strawberry halves and kiwi slices.

Once you have cut out bananas, strawberries, and kiwi, place the shapes on a plate and freeze for 10 to 15 minutes.

While the fruit is in the freezer, melt the chocolate in the microwave or a double boiler.

Remove the fruit from the freezer and dip the fruit shapes into the chocolate using a fork. Tap the side of the bowl to remove excess chocolate and then place on a waxed paper-lined baking sheet. Continue with the remaining fruit.

Once all the fruit is covered with chocolate, transfer to the refrigerator or freezer to allow the chocolate to set. Serve.

The fruit bites are best stored in an airtight container in the freezer. Allow the bites to come to room temperature before enjoying.

MAKES 2 TO 3 DOZEN BITES

Mini Lemon "Cheesecakes" with Raspberries

These little cheesecakes are not like your ordinary cheesecake. The "cheese" is composed of fresh lemon, vanilla, cashews, honey, and coconut oil, giving these cheesecakes the creamiest and smoothest texture. The topping of raspberry and mint makes these little cakes a refreshing go-to spring dessert.

FOR CRUST:

1½ cups (180 g) almond flour

⅓ cup (27 g) unsweetened shredded coconut

4 Medjool dates, pitted and chopped

3 tablespoons (41 ml) extra-virgin unrefined coconut oil, melted

¼ teaspoon sea salt

FOR FILLING:

1½ cups (200 g) raw cashews, soaked in water overnight at room temperature

⅓ cup (80 ml) fresh lemon juice

⅓ cup (75 g) extra-virgin unrefined coconut oil (no need to melt)

¼ cup (80 g) raw honey

1 teaspoon (5 ml) vanilla extract

1 teaspoon (1.7 g) lemon zest

¼ teaspoon sea salt

¼ cup (35 g) fresh raspberries

Fresh mint leaves

To make the crust: Place the almond flour, shredded coconut, dates, coconut oil, and salt in the bowl of a food processor or blender and process until smooth. Spoon about 1 tablespoon (15 g) crust into the bottom of each cup of a mini cheesecake pan and press each portion into the bottom, making sure to cover the bottom evenly. Chill the crusts in the refrigerator while you make the filling.

To make the filling: Drain the cashews and place in the bowl of a food processor with the lemon juice, coconut oil, honey, vanilla extract, lemon zest, and sea salt. Process until smooth, stopping a few times to scrape down the sides of the bowl, 3 to 4 minutes. Divide the mixture evenly among the cheesecake crusts, filling to the top. Chill overnight.

When ready to serve, top with fresh the raspberries and fresh mint leaves.

Place in an airtight container in the refrigerator and enjoy within 3 days.

MAKES 12 MINI CHEESECAKES

Apricot Crumb Cake

Apricots start to show up at the local markets at the end of spring and into the beginning of the summer months. These beautiful orange-colored fruits are a great source of beta-carotene, vitamin C, and fiber. Apricots have a faint tartness and have a sweet flavor between a peach and a plum.

FOR CAKE:

1 cup (120 g) almond flour

¼ cup (30 g) hazelnut flour

2 tablespoons (15 g) coconut flour

1½ teaspoons (2.7 g) ground ginger

½ teaspoon ground cinnamon

½ teaspoon baking soda

¼ teaspoon sea salt

3 eggs

¼ cup (55 g) extra-virgin unrefined coconut oil, melted

1½ tablespoons (30 g) raw honey

1 teaspoon (5 ml) vanilla extract

6 fresh apricots, pitted and chopped

FOR TOPPING:

½ cup (40 g) unsweetened shredded coconut

¼ cup (30 g) almond flour

1 teaspoon (2.3 g) ground cinnamon

2 tablespoons (27 g) extra-virgin unrefined coconut oil, melted

2 tablespoons (40 g) raw honey

Pinch of sea salt

Preheat the oven to 350°F (180°C, or gas mark 4). Grease an 8-inch (20 cm) cake pan with coconut oil and set aside.

To make the cake: In a large bowl, whisk together the almond flour, hazelnut flour, coconut flour, ginger, cinnamon, baking soda, and salt.

In a small bowl, whisk together the eggs, coconut oil, honey, and vanilla. Pour the wet ingredients into the dry ingredients and stir to combine. Add the chopped apricots to the batter and stir to combine.

To make the topping: Combine the coconut, almond flour, cinnamon, coconut oil, honey, and salt in a small bowl and mix together until wet crumbs form. Set aside.

Pour the apricot mixture into the prepared cake pan and sprinkle with the topping mixture to evenly coat.

Bake for 30 to 35 minutes, or until golden and a toothpick inserted into the center comes out clean.

Cover the cake and store in the refrigerator for up to 4 days.

MAKES ONE 8-INCH (20 CM) CAKE

Strawberry Nut Bars

These bars are a refreshing springtime dessert enhanced by freshly picked sweet strawberries. My family has been known to enjoy these bars as a breakfast treat, too. Feel free to substitute other berries such as raspberries, blueberries, or blackberries to these bars—just reduce the amount of strawberries and enjoy!

1½ cups (263 g) pitted and chopped Medjool dates

¼ cup (25 g) pecans, lightly toasted

2 tablespoons (15 g) almond flour

2 tablespoons (40 g) raw honey, divided

1¼ teaspoons ground cinnamon, divided

¼ teaspoon sea salt

1 cup (150 g) strawberries sliced lengthwise, divided

¼ teaspoon ground ginger

¼ cup sliced almonds, lightly toasted (see Note)

Line a 9 x 5-inch (23 x 12.5 cm) loaf pan with parchment paper, allowing the paper to go up the sides.

In the bowl of a food processor, combine the dates, pecans, almond flour, 1 tablespoon of the honey, 1 teaspoon of the cinnamon, and salt and pulse until combined and the mixture forms a slightly crumbly dough.

Press the date mixture into the bottom of the loaf pan and refrigerate for 5 minutes.

Meanwhile, in a small bowl, combine ½ cup (75 g) of the strawberries, the remaining 1 tablespoon (20 g) honey, remaining ¼ teaspoon cinnamon, and ginger. With the back of a fork, mash the strawberry mixture until the berries are smashed and everything is combined. Spread the strawberry mixture on top of the date mixture.

Arrange the remaining ½ cup (75 g) sliced strawberries on top of the strawberry mash. Sprinkle the almond slices over the strawberries. Refrigerate the bars for 10 minutes, to set up. Release the bars by pulling up on the sides of the parchment paper. Then slice the bars into squares and serve.

The bars are great served alone or with a dollop of coconut whipped cream (page 32). The bars are best stored in the refrigerator for up to 4 days.

MAKES SIX 3 X 2½-INCH (7.6 X 6.4 CM) BARS

Note: To toast the almonds (and other nuts), spread them in an even, single layer on a rimmed baking sheet. Bake in a 350°F (180°C, or gas mark 4) oven for 5 to 10 minutes, or until golden, stirring once.

Chocolate-Apricot Bars

These are a great option for snack bars for my little ones or to pack in their lunch box. They are naturally sweetened by the fruit in the bars, so they are better options than some of the packaged bars out there. Just wrap the bars individually in parchment paper and place inside individual snack bags.

1 cup (130 g) pitted and chopped dried apricots

½ cup (88 g) pitted and chopped Medjool dates

¼ cup (27 g) sliced almonds, lightly toasted (see Note, page 48)

¼ cup (27 g) chopped pecans, lightly toasted (see Note, page 48)

3½ tablespoons (18 g) unsweetened shredded coconut, divided

1½ tablespoons (22 ml) maple syrup

½ teaspoon ground cinnamon

½ teaspoon ground ginger

¼ teaspoon sea salt

½ ounce (14 g) dark chocolate (85% cacao or higher), melted

Line a 9 x 5-inch (23 x 12.5 cm) loaf pan with parchment paper, allowing the paper to hang over the sides of the pan.

In the bowl of a food processor, pulse together the apricots, dates, almonds, pecans, 1½ tablespoons (8 g) of the coconut, maple syrup, cinnamon, ginger, and sea salt until finely ground.

Transfer the mixture to the pan and press firmly into the bottom. Refrigerate for 20 to 30 minutes to set up. Then use the parchment paper overhang to remove the bars from the pan. Drizzle the bars with the melted dark chocolate and sprinkle with remaining 2 tablespoons (10 g) coconut.

Refrigerator the bars for 10 to 15 minutes, or until the bars are firm and the chocolate is set. Slice into 6 bars.

The bars can be kept in an airtight container for up to 4 days. They can also be frozen and then brought to room temperature before enjoying.

MAKES 6 BARS

Banana Split Ice Cream

This ice cream wraps all the flavors of a banana split into one scoop of ice cream. Top your ice cream with additional strawberries and chopped pineapple or eat as is. Either way, it's a nice treat without the guilt of a traditional banana split.

2 egg yolks

3 tablespoons (45 ml) maple syrup

1 can (13½ ounces, or 400 ml) coconut milk

½ teaspoon vanilla extract

1 cup (145 g) diced strawberries, plus more for serving

½ cup (75 g) diced banana (about 1 small banana)

2 ounces (56 g) dark chocolate (85% cacao or higher), finely chopped

Prepare a double boiler by setting a glass bowl over a pot of simmering water, but do not let the bowl touch the water. Add the egg yolks and maple syrup to the bowl and stir to warm. Stir the mixture for about 5 minutes. It should become smooth and shiny. Add the coconut milk and whisk everything to combine. As everything warms, it will get smoother. The custard will start to thicken a bit. Stir in the vanilla, turn off the heat, strain through a fine-mesh strainer into a bowl to remove any egg bits, then transfer the bowl to the refrigerator to cool completely.

Add the coconut mixture to your ice cream maker and follow the manufacturer's instructions. At about 75 percent finished, add the strawberries, banana, and chocolate.

Transfer to a container and freeze until firm.

When ready to serve, allow the ice cream to sit out for 5 to 10 minutes to soften to make it easier to scoop. Serve topped with diced fresh strawberries.

Store the ice cream in an airtight container and place in the freezer for up to 3 weeks.

MAKES ABOUT 1 QUART (570 G)

♥

chapter four

SUMMER'S BOUNTY:
BRIGHT, FRUITY FLAVORS

Warm, sunny days and long, light evenings mark the much-loved summer months. Summer is perhaps the best time for seasonal baking due to the range of amazing fruits and vegetables. Each is quenching and cooling—just what is needed on hot sunny days. Juicy peaches, tangy cherries, melons of all sizes, and berries of every color are some of the joys of summer seasonal eating. You'll never find them as fresh and flavorful as they are when they are bought in season at their best. The recipes in this chapter are a great way to enjoy summer's bounty.

- **Peaches:** Peaches are a delicious fruit, with a fuzzy, reddish yellow skin and white or yellow flesh. They are juicy and sweet and at times have a tart taste—and the best aroma that reminds you of hot summer days. This summertime fruit is best between the months of May and September. To select, look for peaches that are firm, with a taut, unblemished skin and no signs of bruising or wrinkles. If you can smell their luscious aroma, you know they are ripe and ready to enjoy.

- **Cherries:** Cherries are amazing in many ways—their sweet and tart flavor can transform a dessert in seconds. Then there are their health-benefiting nutrients and unique antioxidants. Combine them with the antioxidants in dark chocolate in the Dark Chocolate Pots de Crème with Roasted Cherries (page 66) and you have a powerhouse dessert. Cherry season is from the end of May until August. Keep in mind that fresh ripe cherries have a short shelf life, so use them quickly to benefit from all they have to offer.

- **Raspberries:** These bright red fruits are among the most popular berries grown. They are a rich source of health-promoting nutrients, minerals, and vitamins that are essential for optimal health. The goal when purchasing this delightful fruit is to choose berries that are ripe without being overly so. Like cherries, raspberries have an extremely short shelf life, so make sure you use them quickly. The combination of dark chocolate and raspberries is pretty heavenly; see for yourself in the Chocolate-Raspberry Tarts on page 55.

- **Blueberries:** Of all the popular summer fruits, blueberries are the winners when it comes to their nutritional offering. They earn top marks as a potent source of antioxidants, fiber, and vitamin C. To pick the best of the crop, look for powder-blue berries that are firm and uniform in size. Store them in a single layer, if possible, in a moisture-proof container for up to 5 days, and don't wash until you are ready to use them.

Chocolate-Raspberry Tartlets

These no-bake tartlets are a chocolate lover's dream. The fresh raspberries paired with the silky raw cacao filling is a little bite of heaven and will leave your friends and family questioning how this could be Paleo.

||||||||||||||||||||||||||||||||||||||||||||||||||||||||||||||||||||||||||||||||||||||||||||||||||||||||||||||||||||||||||||||||||||||||||||||

FOR CRUST:

1¼ cups (150 g) almond flour

3 tablespoons (24 g) cacao powder

⅛ teaspoon sea salt

2 tablespoons (30 ml) maple syrup

¼ cup (55 g) extra-virgin unrefined coconut oil, melted

FOR RASPBERRY FILLING:

2 cups (270 g) raspberries

2 teaspoons (10 ml) maple syrup

1 teaspoon (5 ml) lemon juice

½ teaspoon ground cinnamon

Pinch of sea salt

FOR CHOCOLATE FILLING:

½ cup (109 ml) extra-virgin unrefined coconut oil, melted

⅓ cup (80 ml) maple syrup

1 cup (120 g) cacao powder

1 cup (135 g) raspberries, for garnish

Thoroughly grease 4 tartlet pans, 5 inches (12.5 cm) each, with coconut oil.

To make the crust: Place the almond flour, cacao powder, and salt into a large bowl and whisk to combine. Add the maple syrup and coconut oil and blend together with a fork until everything comes together and the mixture becomes wet.

Form the dough into 4 small balls and press evenly into the tartlet pans along the bottom and up the sides. Refrigerate for 1 to 2 hours to allow the dough to firm and chill.

To make the raspberry filling: In a nonreactive saucepan over medium heat, add the raspberries, maple syrup, lemon juice, cinnamon, and salt. Constantly stir the raspberry mixture, breaking up the raspberries. Continue to stir for 3 to 4 minutes, until the raspberry mixture starts to thicken and reduce. Remove from the heat and allow to cool for 10 to 15 minutes. When the crust has chilled, spread an even layer of the raspberry mixture on the bottoms of the crusts. Return to the refrigerator while making the chocolate filling.

To make the chocolate filling: Add the coconut oil and maple syrup to the bowl of a food processor and process until well combined. Add the cacao powder and process until smooth, stopping to scrape down the edges of the bowl as needed. Pour the chocolate mixture over the raspberry filling and spread evenly over the top.

Return the tartlets to the refrigerator to set and firm for at least 1 hour. Before serving, allow the tartlets to come to room temperature and then place an even layer of raspberries over the chocolate.

The tartlets can be kept in an airtight container in the refrigerator for up to 4 days.

MAKES 4 TARTLETS

Peach Tart

Peaches, with their soft skin and sweet flesh, are a summertime staple. They provide a great deal of nutrients, too: good-for-you vitamin A, important for healthy vision, and vitamin C, a great antioxidant.

||||||||||||||||||||||||||||||||||||||||||||||||||||||||||||||||||||||||||||||||||

FOR CRUST:

2 cups (240 g) almond flour

¼ cup (30 g) coconut flour

1 teaspoon (2.3 g) ground cinnamon

½ teaspoon unflavored gelatin

¼ teaspoon sea salt

2 Medjool dates, pitted

1 tablespoon (20 g) raw honey

⅓ cup (73 g) extra-virgin unrefined coconut oil, melted

FOR FILLING:

3 or 4 peaches, thinly sliced

2 teaspoons (14 g) raw honey

2 teaspoons (10 ml) fresh lemon juice

2 teaspoons (10 ml) vanilla extract

1 teaspoon (2.6 g) coconut flour

½ teaspoon ground cinnamon

Pinch of sea salt

Preheat the oven to 350°F (180°C, or gas mark 4).

To make the crust: Place the almond flour, coconut flour, cinnamon, gelatin, and salt in the bowl of a food processor and pulse to combine. Add the dates, honey, and coconut oil and process again until a dough forms. Press the dough on the bottom and up the sides of a 9-inch (23 cm) tart pan. Place the crust in the refrigerator to chill for 30 minutes.

To make the filling: In a medium bowl, gently stir together the peaches, honey, lemon juice, vanilla, coconut flour, cinnamon, and salt. Lay the peach slices decoratively in the crust and bake for 30 to 35 minutes, or until the crust is golden and the filling sets.

Let the tart cool completely before serving.

Serve with Vanilla Coconut Ice Cream (page 141) and toasted pecans, or topping of choice.

The tart is best stored in the refrigerator up to 4 days.

MAKES ONE 9-INCH (23 CM) TART

Cinnamon Peach Ice Cream

Growing up in Georgia, I knew it was summer when the fresh peaches hit the market stands. It seemed my grandmother would stop at the local farm stand and buy them in bulk. She knew I loved them, but it was also a tradition to make peach ice cream with them. There was something about having a big scoop of peach ice cream on a hot Georgia summer day.

||||||||||||||||||||||||||||||||||||||||||||||||||||||||||||||||||||||||||||||||||||||||||||||||||||||||||||||||||||

1 can (13 ½ ounces, or 400 ml) coconut milk

3 egg yolks

3 tablespoons (45 ml) maple syrup, divided

1 teaspoon (15 ml) vanilla extract

1½ teaspoons (3.5 g) ground cinnamon, divided

2 ripe peaches, diced, plus more for topping

Combine the coconut milk, egg yolks, 2 tablespoons (30 ml) of the maple syrup, vanilla, and 1 teaspoon (2.3 g) of the cinnamon in a small saucepan. Over low heat, bring to a low boil, while whisking, 4 to 5 minutes, until the mixture thickens and coats the back of a spoon.

Remove from the heat and let cool. Strain the mixture into a medium bowl, cover with plastic wrap, and refrigerate for 2 hours.

While the mixture is in the refrigerator, place the diced peaches, remaining 1 tablespoon (15 ml) maple syrup, and remaining ½ teaspoon cinnamon in a small saucepan over medium heat. Stir until the peaches soften slightly, 2 to 3 minutes.

Remove from the heat and allow to cool.

Place the chilled coconut milk mixture into an ice cream maker and follow the manufacturer's directions until the desired consistency is almost reached. About 5 minutes before it's completed, pour the peach mixture into the ice cream and continue to process.

Serve right away or keep in an airtight container in the freezer for up to 2 weeks and serve when ready. Top with additional peaches and cinnamon for an extra touch and enjoy!

MAKES 1 PINT (285 G)

Banana Blueberry Ice Cream with Coconut Crumble

Homemade ice cream is firmer than store-bought ice cream because store-bought is made with granulated white sugar, fat, stabilizers, and additives, and because homemade can't be churned as heavily as commercial ice cream can be. To serve, simply allow the ice cream to soften on the counter for about 5 minutes, until it's scoop-able.

|||||||||||||||||||||||||||||||||||||||||||||||||||||||||||||||||||||||||||||||||||||||||||||||||||||||||||||||

FOR ICE CREAM:

3 egg yolks

1 can (13½ ounces, or 400 g) coconut milk

1 tablespoon (15 ml) maple syrup

1½ cups (225 g) fresh blueberries, divided

1 ripe banana, mashed (about ½ cup [112 g])

1 teaspoon (5 ml) vanilla extract

FOR COCONUT CRUMBLE:

⅓ cup (40 g) almond flour

⅓ cup (100 g) roughly chopped pecans (or nut of choice)

½ cup (40 g) unsweetened shredded coconut

1 teaspoon (2.3 g) ground cinnamon

¼ teaspoon baking soda

¼ teaspoon sea salt

2 tablespoons (27 ml) extra-virgin unrefined coconut oil, melted

1½ tablespoons (22 g) coconut butter, melted

1 tablespoon (15 ml) maple syrup

1 teaspoon (5 ml) vanilla extract

Fresh blueberries, for topping (optional)

To make the ice cream: Combine the egg yolks, coconut milk, and maple syrup in a saucepan over low heat and bring to a low boil while whisking. Allow the mixture to heat for 4 to 5 minutes after reaching a low boil and continue to whisk. Remove from the heat and let cool for 10 minutes.

In a food processor, add the coconut milk mixture, 1 cup (150 g) of the blueberries, banana, and vanilla. Purée until just combined, 1 to 2 minutes, stopping the processor every 30 seconds to scrape down sides of the bowl with a rubber spatula. Pour the mixture into a large bowl and chill in the refrigerator for 2 hours.

Place the mixture in an ice cream maker, and follow the manufacturer's directions until the desired consistency is reached. Add the remaining ½ cup (75 g) of blueberries 5 minutes before it is completed.

To make the crumble: Preheat the oven to 350°F (180°C, or gas mark 4). In a large bowl, whisk together the almond flour, nuts, coconut, cinnamon, baking soda, and salt. Add the coconut oil and use your fingers or a fork to incorporate the mixture until it resembles coarse crumbs. Add the coconut butter, maple syrup, and vanilla, stirring until just combined and the mixture forms a loose crumble.

Scatter the dough into an 8 x 8-inch (20 x 20 cm) baking dish, pressing evenly into the bottom of the dish. Bake for 10 to 15 minutes, or until golden brown. Let cool completely, and then crumble into small pieces.

To serve, allow the ice cream to soften at room temperature for about 5 minutes. Scoop ½ cup (70 g) ice cream into each bowl and top with 3 tablespoons (42 g) crumble and additional fresh blueberries.

The ice cream is best stored in the freezer for up to 3 weeks.

MAKES ABOUT 1 PINT (285 G) ICE CREAM AND ABOUT 1 CUP (225 G) CRUMBLE

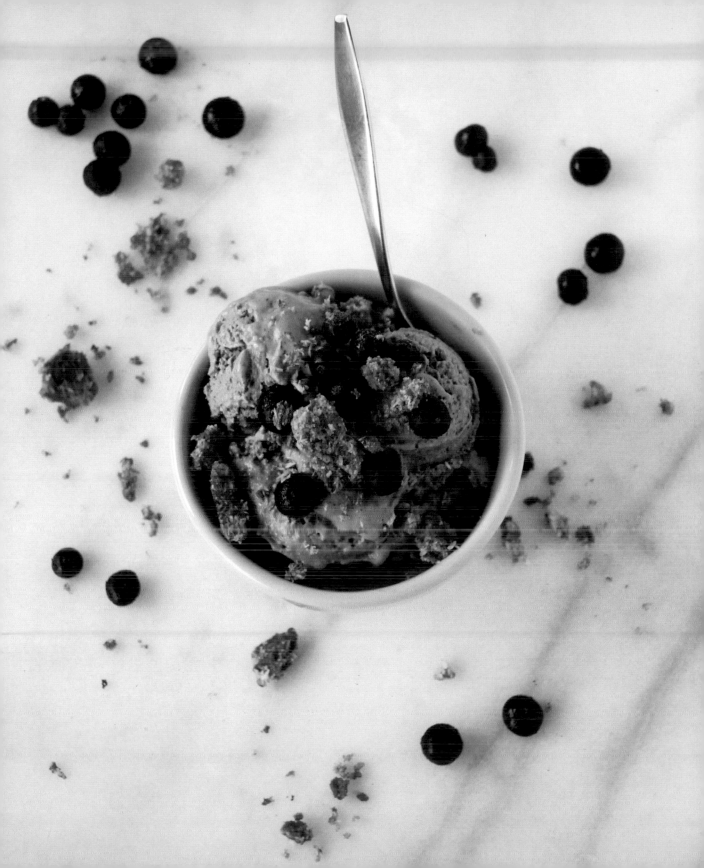

Chocolate Zucchini Cake with Vanilla Spiced Cream

Birthdays come once a year. Why not make them special with a three-layer chocolate cake? The zucchini adds moisture to the cake, which makes it even more decadent.

||||||||||||||||||||||||||||||||||||||||||||||||||||||||||||||||||||||||||||||||||||||||||||||||||||||||||||||||||||||||||||||||||||||||||

FOR CAKE:

8 Medjool dates, pitted

1 tablespoon (15 ml) water

9 eggs

½ cup (109 g) extra-virgin unrefined coconut oil, melted

½ cup (125 g) unsweetened applesauce

2 tablespoons (30 ml) maple syrup

2 teaspoons (10 ml) vanilla extract

¾ cup (180 ml) coconut milk

1 cup (120 g) coconut flour

½ cup (60 g) cacao powder

1 teaspoon (4.6 g) baking soda

1 teaspoon (2.3 g) ground cinnamon

½ teaspoon ground ginger

½ teaspoon sea salt

1¼ cups (138 g) shredded zucchini

FOR VANILLA SPICED CREAM:

2 cups (270 g) raw cashews, soaked in water overnight

1 cup (235 ml) canned coconut milk

2 Medjool dates, pitted

1½ tablespoons (22 ml) maple syrup

¼ teaspoon ground ginger

¼ teaspoon ground cinnamon

1 vanilla bean, split lengthwise, seeds scraped, and pod discarded

FOR TOPPING:

Dark chocolate shavings (optional)

Preheat the oven to 350°F (180°C, or gas mark 4). Grease three 8-inch (20 cm) round cake pans or two 9-inch (23 cm) round cake pans with coconut oil and lightly dust with coconut flour.

To make the cakes: Place the Medjool dates in a microwave-safe bowl with the water and heat on high for 30 seconds. Drain some of the water, leaving about 1 tablespoon (15 ml), then use a fork to mash the dates until smooth.

Place the Medjool dates in a food processor along with the eggs, coconut oil, applesauce, maple syrup, vanilla, and coconut milk and process until smooth.

In a separate bowl, whisk together the coconut flour, cacao powder, baking soda, cinnamon, ginger, and salt.

Add the dry ingredients to the bowl of the food processor with the date mixture and process until well combined, stopping to scrape down the sides of the bowl.

Remove the blade from the food processor and stir in the zucchini.

Evenly distribute the batter among the prepared cake pans and bake for 20 to 22 minutes, or until a toothpick inserted into the center comes out clean. Allow the cakes to cool for 10 minutes before removing from the pan. Transfer the cakes to a wire rack to cool completely.

To make the cream: Drain the cashews. In a food processor, combine the cashews, coconut milk, dates, maple syrup, ginger, cinnamon, and vanilla bean seeds and process until very smooth.

Spread the cream on the top of one of the cooled cakes, just coating the top. Gently place the second cake layer on top of the cream layer. Repeat with the third cake, if using. Then spread additional cream on the top of third cake. Sprinkle the dark chocolate shavings on top of the cake.

The cake can be stored in the refrigerator, covered, for up to 3 days.

MAKES ONE 8-INCH (20 CM) THREE-LAYER OR 9-INCH (23 CM) TWO-LAYER CAKE

Cinnamon Blueberry Cookie Sandwiches

Blueberries have one of the highest antioxidant capacities among all fruits, vegetables, spices, and seasonings. The best way to benefit from their health benefits is to eat them raw. The filling of these cookies allows you to do just that. You can bake the cookies and make the filling a day ahead.

||||||||||||||||||||||||||||||||||||||||||||||||||||||||||||||||||||||||||||||||||||||||||||||||||||||||||

FOR COOKIES:

1¾ cups (210 g) almond flour

2 tablespoons (27 ml) extra-virgin unrefined coconut oil, melted

2 tablespoons (30 ml) maple syrup

1 Medjool date, pitted and chopped

1 tablespoon (15 ml) canned coconut milk

1 teaspoon (5 ml) vanilla extract

1 teaspoon (2.3 g) ground cinnamon

½ teaspoon baking soda

½ teaspoon unflavored gelatin

Pinch of sea salt

FOR BLUEBERRY FILLING:

1 cup (135 g) raw cashews, soaked in water overnight, water discarded

2 Medjool dates, pitted

1 tablespoon (20 g) raw honey

1 teaspoon (5 ml) vanilla extract

⅓ cup (50 g) blueberries

1 tablespoon (15 ml) fresh lemon juice

2 tablespoons (30 ml) canned coconut milk

Preheat the oven to 350°F (180°C, or gas mark 4). Line a baking sheet with parchment paper and set aside.

To make the cookies: In the bowl of a food processor, add the almond flour, coconut oil, maple syrup, date, coconut milk, vanilla, cinnamon, baking soda, gelatin, and salt and process until the dough comes together and forms a ball.

Place a piece of parchment paper on a counter and dust with coconut flour. Place the dough on the parchment paper and dust with additional coconut flour. Place another piece of parchment paper on top of the dough and roll the dough out to ¼-inch (6 mm) thick. Remove the top layer of parchment paper. Cut out 20 cookies with a cookie cutter of choice and carefully place on the prepared baking sheet. Bake the cookies for 10 to 12 minutes, rotating the pan halfway through, or until golden around the edges.

Allow the cookies to cool for 5 to 10 minutes on the baking sheet before transferring to a wire rack to cool completely.

To make the filling: In the bowl of the food processor, add the cashews, dates, honey, vanilla, blueberries, lemon juice, and coconut milk and process until the mixture is smooth, stopping several times to scrape down the sides of the bowl. Add an extra tablespoon (15 ml) coconut milk if the mixture is not becoming smooth.

To assemble, turn one of the cookies over with the bottom up. Scoop 1 tablespoon (16 g) filling onto the top of the cookie and take another cookie with the bottom down and slightly press together. Continue with the remaining cookies to form 10 cookie sandwiches.

The cookies are best enjoyed immediately but can be stored in the refrigerator for up to 2 days.

MAKES ABOUT 10 COOKIE SANDWICHES, DEPENDING ON COOKIE CUTTER

Chocolate Cherry Drop Cookies

Cherries, rich dark chocolate, and the crunch of almonds make these succulent cookies a winner. You can enjoy these cookies year-round if you like by using pitted chopped fresh cherries in season and dried cherries in the off-season.

¾ cup (90 g) almond flour

¼ cup (30 g) cacao powder

½ teaspoon baking soda

½ teaspoon unflavored gelatin

½ teaspoon ground cinnamon

¼ teaspoon sea salt

4 ounces (112 g) dark chocolate (85% cacao or higher), chopped

5 tablespoons (68 g) extra-virgin unrefined coconut oil, melted

¼ cup (60 ml) maple syrup

1 teaspoon (5 ml) vanilla extract

1 egg

¼ cup (28 g) roughly chopped almonds

¼ cup (39 g) fresh (or dried) cherries, pitted and finely chopped

Preheat the oven to 350°F (180°C, or gas mark 4) and line a baking sheet with parchment paper.

In a medium bowl, whisk together the almond flour, cacao, baking soda, gelatin, cinnamon, and salt.

Prepare a double boiler by setting a glass bowl over a pot of simmering water, but do not let the bowl touch the water. Add the dark chocolate and coconut oil to the glass bowl, and stir until melted. Add the melted chocolate mixture to the dry ingredients along with the maple syrup, vanilla, and egg. Mix until well incorporated. Stir in the almonds and cherries.

Using your hands, form the dough into sixteen 1-tablespoon (14 g) balls. Place on the prepared baking sheet and gently press down with your fingers to slightly flatten. Repeat with the remaining batter, spacing the cookies about 2 inches (5 cm) apart.

Bake for 9 to 11 minutes, until the tops of the cookies begin to slightly crack. Remove from the oven and let cool on the baking sheet for 10 minutes before removing to a wire rack to cool completely.

The cookies can be stored in an airtight container in a cool, dry place for up to 2 days. They may also be frozen for up to 2 weeks. If frozen, bring to room temperature before enjoying.

MAKES 16 COOKIES

Dark Chocolate Pots de Crème with Roasted Cherries

The sweet and tangy cherries flavor these rich dark chocolate custards. The French pots de crème or pot-au-crème translates as "pot of cream," because this dessert is served in small lidded porcelain pots—but you can use ramekins, jars, or custard cups. It is particularly important to bake these custards in a water bath, which insulates them from the harsh heat of the oven.

4 ounces (112 g) cherries, pitted and cut in half (or quarters, if large)

¼ to ½ teaspoon ground cinnamon

2 cups (470 ml) canned coconut milk

1 vanilla bean, split lengthwise, seeds scraped, and pod retained

1 egg

2 egg yolks

4 ounces (112 g) dark chocolate, finely chopped

Pinch of sea salt

Preheat the oven to 425°F (220°C, or gas mark 7).

Place the cherries in an 8-inch (20 cm) baking dish and sprinkle with the cinnamon. Roast for 20 to 30 minutes, until the cherries are very soft. Set the cherries aside to cool while you prepare the pots de crème.

Lower the oven temperature to 300°F (150°C, or gas mark 2).

In a medium saucepan over medium heat, combine the coconut milk, vanilla bean seeds, and vanilla bean and bring to a low simmer.

In a small bowl, whisk together the egg and egg yolks. When the coconut milk has come to a simmer, remove the pan from the heat and remove the vanilla pod. Add the chocolate to the milk mixture and stir to melt. Slowly whisk the egg mixture into the chocolate and milk mixture. Strain the mixture through a fine-mesh strainer into a clean bowl.

Chop the roasted cherries and stir into the chocolate mixture (along with juices) with the sea salt.

Pour the mixture into four 6-ounce, (168 g) oven-safe ramekins or jars. Place the ramekins in a deep baking pan and place the pan in the oven. Add enough hot tap water around the pan to come halfway up the sides of the ramekins.

Bake the custards for 30 to 40 minutes, or until the center is set. Let the ramekins cool to room temperature.

They can be served at room temperature or chilled and served with the topping of choice.

MAKES 4 SERVINGS

Summer Fruit Parfaits

Ripe, fresh summer fruits layered with freshly whipped coconut cream make a deceptively simple dessert. Mint and lemon zest add another flavor dimension to the seasonal mix of fruits.

|||||||||||||||||||||||||||||||||||||||||||||||||||||||||||||||||||||||||||||||||||||||||||||||||||||||||||||||||||||||||||||||||

FOR FRUIT:

1 nectarine, pitted and thinly sliced

8 strawberries, sliced

1 peach, pitted and thinly sliced

1 teaspoon (1.7 g) grated lemon zest

¼ cup (80 g) raw honey

1 kiwifruit, peeled

1 cup (145 g) blueberries

FOR COCONUT WHIPPED CREAM:

2 cans (13½ ounces, or 400 ml each) coconut milk, refrigerated overnight

1 tablespoon (15 ml) maple syrup

½ teaspoon vanilla extract

4 fresh mint sprigs, leaves removed and chopped, for garnish

To prepare the fruit: In a wide, shallow dish, arrange the nectarine slices in a single layer. Arrange the strawberry slices over the nectarine slices. Arrange the peach slices over the berries. Sprinkle the lemon zest evenly over the fruit, then drizzle with the honey. Set aside, covered, for 1 to 2 hours at room temperature. During this time the fruits will release more juices, which will mix with the honey to form a light syrup.

Halve the kiwifruit lengthwise. Cut each half crosswise into slices. Add the kiwi slices and blueberries to the prepared fruit and, using a spoon, gently mix all the fruits to coat evenly with the syrup.

To make the whipped cream: Open the cans of coconut milk without shaking or turning upside down. Carefully spoon out the layer of thick coconut cream at the top and add to a mixing bowl.

Add the maple syrup and vanilla to the coconut cream, along with any additional flavorings of choice, such as cinnamon, ginger, or almond extract instead of vanilla.

With a hand mixer on low speed, whip the coconut milk until creamy, moving to a higher speed after a couple of minutes. Mix for about 5 minutes, or until you have thick, whipped peaks.

To assemble each parfait, use a slotted spoon to scoop about ¼ cup (60 g) of the fruit, pausing to allow it to drain well over the dish, and place the fruit in a single-serving parfait glass or the bottom of a balloon wineglass. Spoon ⅓ cup (15 g) of the whipped cream over the fruit in an even layer. Scoop up ½ cup (120 g) of the fruit, again making sure it is well drained, and arrange it on top of the whipped cream. Layer another ⅓ cup (15 g) of whipped cream on top. Finally, place ¼ cup (60 g) well-drained fruit in the center. Repeat to make 3 more parfaits.

Garnish each parfait with chopped mint leaves and serve immediately, or cover with plastic wrap and refrigerate for up to 2 hours.

Parfaits are best enjoyed the day they're made.

MAKES 4 SERVINGS

Peach Berry Spiced Cookie Crumble

Growing up in Georgia as a little girl, I knew it was summer when the fresh peaches would grace the local market stand by my grandmother's house. I would be so excited to get my hands on one—or even more, to take a bite of my grandmother's peach cobbler, which was a tradition in her kitchen. This crumble is my take on a peach cobbler but allows the sweetness of the fresh summer fruits to do all the work.

FOR FILLING:

2 ripe reaches, pitted and diced

2 cups (290 g) blueberries

1 cup (135 g) raspberries

1 tablespoon (20 g) raw honey or (15 ml) maple syrup

2 tablespoons (30 ml) lemon juice

¼ teaspoon ground cinnamon

¼ teaspoon ground ginger

1½ teaspoons (4 g) coconut flour

FOR TOPPING:

20 Spiced Cookie Cutter Cookies (page 164)

¼ cup (25 g) almond meal

¼ cup (20 g) unsweetened shredded coconut

½ cup (75 g) coarsely chopped pecans

3 Medjool dates, pitted and diced

1 tablespoon (15 ml) maple syrup

1 teaspoon (2.3 g) ground cinnamon

½ teaspoon sea salt

⅓ cup (73 g) extra-virgin unrefined coconut oil, melted

Preheat the oven to 350°F (180°C, or gas mark 4) and grease four 6-ounce, (168 g) oven-safe ramekins or one 9-inch (23 cm) baking dish with coconut oil.

To make the filling: In a large mixing bowl, gently stir together the peaches, berries, honey, lemon juice, cinnamon, and ginger. Sprinkle the coconut flour over the peach and berry mixture and gently fold to combine. Spoon the fruit mixture into the ramekins or baking dish.

To make the topping: In a large bowl, crush the cookies with a fork or your fingers so that they are halfway mashed, leaving some big chunks of cookies. Stir in the almond meal, coconut, pecans, dates, maple syrup, cinnamon, and salt to combine. Add the coconut oil to the mixture and stir to evenly incorporate.

Generously top each ramekin with the cookie topping and bake for 30 to 40 minutes, or until golden brown and bubbling at the edges. Let cool for 5 minutes before serving. Best served with Vanilla Coconut Ice Cream (page 141).

Cover and store in the refrigerator for up to 3 days.

MAKES FOUR 6-OUNCE, (168 G) RAMEKINS OR ONE 9-INCH, (23 CM) PAN

Raspberry Thumbprint Cookies

Growing up, I adored the traditional thumbprint cookies that graced the cookie jar. I thought when switching to a grain-free and refined sugar–free way of life, these cookies would no longer be in my life. I was wrong! Enjoy these cookies with different fillings throughout the year. During the holidays, my kids and I like to fill them with melted dark chocolate for a more decadent treat.

||||||||||||||||||||||||||||||||||||||||||||||||||||||||||||||||||||||||||||||||||||||||||||||||||||||||||||||||||||||||||||

FOR COOKIES:

1 cup (120 g) hazelnut meal

1 cup (120 g) almond flour

3 tablespoons (22 g) coconut flour

½ teaspoon ground cinnamon

¼ teaspoon ground ginger

½ teaspoon unflavored gelatin

½ teaspoon sea salt

¼ cup (60 ml) maple syrup

½ cup (109 ml) extra-virgin unrefined coconut oil, melted

FOR FILLING:

1 cup (135 g) raspberries

1 teaspoon (5 ml) maple syrup

1 teaspoon (5 ml) fresh lemon juice

¼ teaspoon ground cinnamon

1 ounce (28 g) dark chocolate (85% cacao or higher), melted

Preheat the oven to 350°F (180°C, or gas mark 4). Line a baking sheet with parchment paper and set aside.

To make the cookies: In the bowl of a food processor, combine the hazelnut meal, almond flour, coconut flour, cinnamon, ginger, gelatin, and salt and pulse until combined. Add the maple syrup and coconut oil and process until incorporated.

Using your hands, roll the dough to form fifteen 1½-inch (3.8 cm) balls. Place the balls onto the prepared baking sheet and transfer to the refrigerator for 10 minutes to chill.

Remove the balls from the refrigerator and, using your index finger, gently press into the center of the cookies to form an indentation. Bake the cookies for 10 to 12 minutes, or until the cookies are golden brown around the edges. Cool on the baking sheet for 5 to 10 minutes and then transfer to a wire rack to cool completely.

To make the filling: While the cookies bake, heat a nonreactive saucepan over medium heat. Add the raspberries, maple syrup, lemon juice, and cinnamon. Constantly stir the mixture until the raspberries are broken up and the mixture starts to thicken, 4 to 5 minutes. Remove from the heat and allow the filling to cool.

Spoon a teaspoon of raspberry filling into the center of each cookie. Then drizzle dark chocolate over the tops of the cookies. Allow the chocolate to set before serving.

The cookies are best stored in an airtight container in the refrigerator for up to 4 days.

MAKES 15 COOKIES

Lemon-Blueberry Bundt Cake

The zingy lemon and fresh sweet blueberries in this cake marry to create one of my favorite summertime recipes. This cake is a great option to add to your summer brunch menu or even for a light and refreshing dessert on a hot summer night. For the lemon zest in this recipe, I always recommend using an organic lemon free of chemicals and pesticides that might reside deep in the rind.

8 Medjool dates, pitted

8 eggs

2 teaspoons (10 ml) vanilla extract

1 tablespoon (15 ml) lemon juice

2 teaspoons (3.5 g) lemon zest

½ cup (120 ml) canned coconut milk

⅓ cup (73 g) extra-virgin unrefined coconut oil, melted

¾ cup (90 g) coconut flour

½ cup (60 g) hazelnut flour

1 teaspoon (2.3 g) unflavored gelatin

1 teaspoon (4.6 g) baking soda

½ teaspoon sea salt

½ teaspoon ground cinnamon

½ teaspoon ground ginger

1 cup (145 g) blueberries

Preheat the oven to 350°F (180°C, or gas mark 4). Grease a Bundt pan with coconut oil and dust with coconut flour. Set aside.

In the bowl of a food processor, add the dates, eggs, vanilla, lemon juice, lemon zest, coconut milk, and coconut oil and process until smooth and the dates are broken up.

In a small bowl, whisk together the coconut flour, hazelnut flour, gelatin, baking soda, salt, cinnamon, and ginger. Add the dry ingredients to the bowl of the food processor and process until everything is incorporated, stopping to scrape down the sides of the bowl. Remove the blade from the food processor and gently stir in the blueberries. Pour the batter into the prepared Bundt cake pan.

Bake for 40 to 45 minutes, or until golden and a toothpick inserted into the cake comes out clean.

Cool the cake for at least 30 minutes before removing from the pan. After the cake is cooled, turn out onto a plate or cake stand.

Slice and serve.

The cake is best stored in an airtight container in the refrigerator and warmed before serving.

MAKES 1 CAKE

Chocolate Pineapple "Donut" Pops

These are a fun summertime dessert to make with the little ones in your life.
They love helping create their own pops. Feel free to play around with the toppings
for these, too. Make a pineapple pop station so the kids can customize to their liking.
Dip the pineapple and have the kids ready to decorate.

1 pineapple, peeled

**4 ounces (112 g) dark chocolate
(85% cacao or higher)**

**¼ cup (56 g) extra-virgin
unrefined coconut oil**

**¼ cup (20 g) unsweetened
shredded coconut**

¼ cup (28 g) chopped almonds

Line a baking sheet with waxed paper.

Core the pineapple with a pineapple corer and cut into 6 rings or
"donuts" about 1 inch (2.5 cm) thick. (If you don't have a pineapple
corer, slice the pineapple into the rings, then use a small biscuit cutter
or ring mold to cut out the core of each ring.) Place the rings on the
prepared baking sheet. Carefully place a wooden stick through the
center of each pineapple. Transfer the baking sheet to the freezer for
30 to 60 minutes to allow the stick to set in the pineapple.

When ready to make, prepare a double boiler by setting a glass bowl
over a pot of simmering water, but do not let the bowl touch the
water. Melt the dark chocolate and coconut oil in the bowl. Carefully
dip a pineapple pop into the chocolate, transfer back to the waxed
paper, and sprinkle with the coconut and almonds. Continue with the
remaining pineapple pops.

Return to the freezer to allow the chocolate to set, 20 to 30 minutes.

Serve and enjoy.

Pops can be kept in an airtight container and stored in the freezer
and enjoyed for up to 7 days.

MAKES 6 POPS

Fresh Blueberry and Blackberry Crumble

A crispy crumb topping is the perfect match to the blueberry and blackberry filling. These intensely flavored berries are usually at their best during the heat of the summer. Feel free to change up the berries in this crumble based on what berries are your favorite from the season.

|||||||||||||||||||||||||||||||||||||||||||||||||||||||||||||||||||||||||||||||||||||||||||||||||||||||||||||||||||||||||||||||

FOR FILLING:

2 cups (290 g) blueberries

2 cups (290 g) blackberries

1 teaspoon (2.3 g) ground cinnamon

½ teaspoon ground ginger

⅛ teaspoon sea salt

1 tablespoon (15 ml) lemon juice

2 tablespoons (30 ml) maple syrup

1 teaspoon (5 ml) vanilla extract

FOR CRUMBLE TOPPING:

½ cup (60 g) almond flour

¼ cup (28 g) chopped almonds

¼ cup (28 g) chopped pecans

1 teaspoon (2.3 g) ground cinnamon

⅛ teaspoon sea salt

2 tablespoons (27 g) extra-virgin unrefined coconut oil, melted

1 tablespoon (15 ml) maple syrup

Preheat the oven to 350°F (180°C, or gas mark 4). Grease a glass 9 x 9-inch (23 x 23 cm) baking dish with coconut oil.

To make the filling: In a medium saucepan over medium heat, combine the berries, cinnamon, ginger, salt, lemon juice, maple syrup, and vanilla. Bring to a low boil for 5 to 10 minutes, or until the liquid has reduced by half.

To make the crumble topping: In a medium bowl, whisk together the almond flour, almonds, pecans, cinnamon, and salt. Stir in the coconut oil and maple syrup. The mixture will be slightly chunky and crumbly. If too dry, add ½ to 1 tablespoon (8 to 15 ml) more melted coconut oil.

To assemble, pour the berries into the prepared dish. Then, using your fingers, sprinkle the crumble mixture evenly over the top of the berries.

Bake the crumble for 15 to 20 minutes, or until the topping starts to turn golden. Cut into nine 3-inch (7.5 cm) squares. Serve warm with Vanilla Coconut Ice Cream (page 141).

Crumble is best served immediately but can be stored in the refrigerator, covered, for up to 3 days.

MAKES 9 SERVINGS

Cherry Vanilla Spiced Cake

Almond flour, when baked, brings out a naturally sweet and toasted nutty flavor that gives great depth to a dessert. Add cherries to the equation and you have the perfect treat for any celebration—or just to welcome the arrival of summer.

||||||||||||||||||||||||||||||||||||||||||||||||||||||||||||||||||||||||||||||||||||||||||||||||||||||||||||||||||||||||||||

3 cups (360 g) almond flour

1 teaspoon (2.3 g) ground cinnamon

½ teaspoon ground ginger

½ teaspoon baking soda

½ teaspoon unflavored gelatin

¼ teaspoon sea salt

3 eggs

1 teaspoon (5 ml) vanilla extract

½ cup (109 g) ghee or extra-virgin unrefined coconut oil, melted

⅓ cup (80 ml) maple syrup

¼ cup (60 ml) canned coconut milk

1 cup (155 g) pitted and halved cherries

Preheat the oven to 350°F (180°C, or gas mark 4). Grease a Bundt pan or regular 9-inch (23 cm) cake pan with coconut oil and dust with coconut flour.

In a large bowl, whisk together the almond flour, cinnamon, ginger, baking soda, gelatin, and salt.

In a small bowl, using a hand mixer, combine the eggs, vanilla, ghee, maple syrup, and coconut milk. Add the wet ingredients to the bowl of the dry ingredients and mix until everything is incorporated. Gently stir in the cherries to evenly distribute in the batter.

Pour the batter into the prepared cake pan and bake for 25 to 30 minutes, or until golden and a toothpick inserted near the center comes out clean.

Allow the cake to cool for at least 30 minutes before releasing from the pan.

After the cake is cooled, turn out onto a plate or cake stand.

The cake is best stored in an airtight container in the refrigerator for up to 5 days.

MAKES 1 CAKE

Grilled Pineapple Ice Cream Pie

As a child, I visited Hawaii with my family, and ever since, I have loved the sweet taste of pineapple. It takes me back to those beautiful islands and all the wonderful memories created on that trip. This pie is a refreshing and cool treat, especially on a hot summer day.

2 cups (100 g) Graham Cracker crumbs (page 160)

3½ tablespoons (48 ml) extra-virgin unrefined coconut oil, melted

3 dates, pitted and finely chopped

3½ cups (500 g) Vanilla Coconut Ice Cream (page 141)

1 pineapple, peeled, cored, and sliced into ½-inch (1.3 cm) rings

4 ounces (112 g) dark chocolate (85% cacao or higher), melted

Preheat the oven to 350°F (180°C, or gas mark 4).

In the bowl of a food processor, combine the graham cracker crumbs, coconut oil, and dates and process until the mixture forms wet crumbs and the dates are broken up completely. Press the mixture into a 9-inch (23 cm) pie plate, going up the sides of the pie plate. Bake the crust for 12 to 15 minutes, or until golden brown. Allow to cool completely, then spread the ice cream in the crust. Freeze for 4 hours.

Before serving, grill the pineapple slices (be sure to start with a clean, lightly oiled grill pan). Top the pie with hot-from-the-grill pineapple slices and drizzle with the melted dark chocolate. Cut into slices and serve.

Store the pie, covered, in the freezer for up to 1 month. Allow to sit at room temperature for 5 to 10 minutes before cutting and serving.

MAKES ONE 9-INCH (23 CM) PIE

♥

chapter five

AUTUMN'S HARVEST:
A CORNUCOPIA OF SWEET AND SAVORY

Autumn is a glorious time of year. The scorching summer sun has faded, taking with it long sunlit days. With autumn's cooler temperatures, we get a sense of culinary freedom that brings us back inside to heat up the kitchen once again. Even though the weather may be cooler in the autumn months, the produce choices are heating up. There is amazing seasonal produce being harvested, which will make traveling to your local market extra special. Some of autumn's baking favorites include pumpkins, winter squash, apples, pears, and sweet potatoes.

- **Pumpkin:** A staple for autumn festivities, these delightful fruits can be amazingly sweet tasting (as is the case with sugar pumpkins, also called pie pumpkins). They are among the most versatile members of the gourd—winter squash—family, so scout your local farmers' market for varying varieties, including pale peach, light blue, green, and even white pumpkins. If making your own pumpkin purée, look for pumpkins that are small, about 5 pounds (2.3 kg), with tough skin.

- **Winter Squash:** Winter squash comes in many different varieties. While each type varies in shape, color, size, and flavor, they all share some common characteristics. Their shells are hard and difficult to pierce, giving them long storage periods between 1 week and 6 months. Their flesh is mildly sweet in flavor and finely grained in texture. Additionally, all have seeded inner cavities. Just scoop out the seeds—they're excellent toasted. Winter squashes—particularly acorn squash and butternut squash—are at their best from October to November, when they are in peak season.

- **Apples:** Apples are a crisp, white-fleshed fruit with a red, yellow, or green skin. They have a moderately sweet, refreshing flavor and a tartness that is present to greater or lesser degree depending on the variety. For example, Golden and Red Delicious apples are mild and sweet, while Granny Smith apples are notably brisk and tart. Tart apples, which best retain their texture during cooking or baking, are better for desserts like the Baked Crumble-Stuffed Apples (page 101). Delicious apples and other sweeter varieties like Braeburn, Honey Crisp, Fuji, and Gala are usually eaten raw but can be used shredded in the Apple Spice Cakie Cookies (page 83).

Apple Spice Cakie Cookies

I know it's fall when I enter the local farmers' market and I see pumpkins and apples.
These soft, cakelike cookies are sweetened with only apples and dates.

6 Medjool dates, pitted

1½ tablespoons (22 ml) water, divided

½ cup (125 g) unsweetened applesauce

1 tablespoon (14 g) extra-virgin unrefined coconut oil, melted

1 teaspoon (2.3 g) apple pie spice or ground cinnamon, plus more for sprinkling

1 teaspoon (5 ml) vanilla extract

1¼ cups (150 g) almond flour

½ teaspoon baking soda

Pinch of sea salt

½ cup (75 g) shredded apple (about 1 small apple)

Preheat the oven to 350°F (180°C, or gas mark 4). Line a baking sheet with parchment paper and set aside.

In a microwave-safe dish, place the dates and 1 tablespoon (15 ml) of the water and microwave on high for 30 seconds. Remove and mash the dates with a fork. Add the remaining ½ tablespoon (8 ml) water and microwave for another 30 seconds. Remove and mash again.

In the bowl of a food processor, place the date mixture, applesauce, coconut oil, apple pie spice, and vanilla and process until smooth.

In a medium bowl, combine the almond flour, baking soda, and salt. Mix the date mixture into the dry ingredients and stir to combine. Add the shredded apple to the bowl and stir until well incorporated into the batter.

Using an ice cream scoop, scoop the batter into cookie balls and transfer to the prepared baking sheet. Once all the cookies are on the sheet, slightly press down on the tops with damp fingers. Sprinkle with additional apple pie spice or cinnamon. Bake for 20 to 25 minutes, or until golden and cooked through.

The cookies are best stored in an airtight container in the refrigerator for up to 6 days. Cookies may also be frozen for up to 2 months.

MAKES 10 TO 18 COOKIES, DEPENDING ON SIZE OF SCOOP

Pumpkin Pecan Pie Bars

Pumpkin pie is a traditional fall dessert that graces most Thanksgiving tables. These bars are a twist on pumpkin pie with the added pecan topping. Just press the crust into a pie plate and follow the directions for the filling.

FOR CRUST:

1¼ cups (150 g) almond flour

¼ cup (30 g) hazelnut flour

2 tablespoons (30 ml) maple syrup

2 tablespoons (27 g) extra-virgin unrefined coconut oil, melted

1 teaspoon (2.3 g) cinnamon

½ teaspoon ground ginger

¼ teaspoon ground nutmeg

¼ teaspoon ground cloves

¼ teaspoon baking soda

¼ teaspoon sea salt

FOR FILLING:

1¾ cups (429 g) pumpkin purée

2 eggs

5 Medjool dates, pitted

½ cup (120 ml) coconut milk

1 tablespoon (15 ml) vanilla extract

1½ tablespoons (11 g) pumpkin pie spice

FOR TOPPING:

½ cup (60 g) almond flour

½ cup (55 g) pecan halves, chopped

⅓ cup (27 g) unsweetened shredded coconut

1 tablespoon (15 ml) maple syrup

1 Medjool date, pitted and finely chopped

1 tablespoon (14 g) extra-virgin unrefined coconut oil, melted

1 teaspoon (2.3 g) ground cinnamon

Preheat the oven to 350°F (180°C, or gas mark 4). Line an 8 x 8-inch (20 x 20 cm) baking dish with parchment paper, making sure the paper goes up the sides.

To make the crust: In a small bowl, combine the almond flour, hazelnut flour, maple syrup, coconut oil, cinnamon, ginger, nutmeg, cloves, baking soda, and salt. Using a fork, stir together until a crust forms. Press the crust mixture into the prepared baking dish, forming an even layer across the bottom of the pan. Bake the crust for 10 to 15 minutes, or until golden. Allow the crust to cool completely.

To make the filling: In the bowl of food processer or high-speed blender, place the pumpkin purée, eggs, dates, coconut milk, vanilla, and pumpkin pie spice. Process until smooth and the dates are broken up. Pour the filling into the cooled crust.

To make the topping: In a medium bowl, combine the almond flour, pecans, coconut, maple syrup, date, coconut oil, and cinnamon. Mix well, then evenly sprinkle across the filling.

Bake for 40 to 45 minutes, or until the filling is set. Allow the bars to cool completely before removing from the pan, using the parchment paper overhang. Cut into sixteen 2-inch (5 cm) squares.

Store the bars in an airtight container in the refrigerator for up to 4 days. Before enjoying, allow the bars to come to room temperature.

MAKES 16 BARS

Apple Pear Crisp

There are several varieties of apples and pears that are grown especially in the region you live. I like mixing up the types I use for this recipe, depending on what is available from our local farmers. My girls love apples and pears, so I leave it up to them to pick the types when we visit the market. They love being a part of our market visits.

||||||||||||||||||||||||||||||||||||||||||||||||||||||||||||||||||||||||||||||||||||||||||||||||||||||||||||||||||||||||||||||||||||||||||||||||||||||||||||||||||||

FOR FILLING:

2 apples, peeled and cored

2 pears, peeled and cored

Juice of ½ lemon

1½ teaspoons (3.5 g) apple pie spice or ground cinnamon

FOR TOPPING:

1 cup (110 g) chopped pecans

½ cup (60 g) almond flour

2½ tablespoons (34 g) extra-virgin unrefined coconut oil, melted

2 teaspoons (10 ml) vanilla extract

2 teaspoons (10 ml) maple syrup (optional)

2 teaspoons (4.6 g) ground cinnamon

1 teaspoon (1.8 g) ground ginger

¼ teaspoon ground nutmeg

¼ teaspoon ground cloves

Preheat the oven to 350°F (180°C, or gas mark 4).

To make the filling: Cut the apples and pears into small pieces. The size of the pieces will depend on how chunky you prefer your crisp. I prefer the pieces to be chopped small. Place the chopped apples and pears in a small bowl and toss with the lemon juice and apple pie spice.

Pour the apple/pear mixture into an 8 x 8-inch (20 x 20 cm) glass baking dish or into four 6-ounce (169 g) ramekins, about three-fourths full.

To make the topping: In a small bowl, combine the pecans, almond flour, coconut oil, vanilla, maple syrup, cinnamon, ginger, nutmeg, and cloves. Use a fork to blend together. The crumbs should be wet. If they are still dry, add ½ tablespoon (8 ml) melted coconut oil and blend with the fork again.

Sprinkle the topping over the filling. Cover the baking dish or each ramekin with aluminum foil and place on a baking sheet. Bake for 15 to 25 minutes, or until the apples and pears start to bubble. Then remove the foil and bake for an additional 15 to 20 minutes, or until the top is golden.

Allow to cool slightly before serving. Top with Vanilla Coconut Ice Cream (page 141) or other Paleo-friendly ice cream of choice.

The crisp can be covered and stored in the refrigerator for up to 3 days. Reheat before serving.

MAKES 1 LARGE CRISP OR 4 INDIVIDUAL CRISPS

Fall Harvest Cupcakes with Pumpkin Spiced Cream

Autumn is my favorite time of year. When the air turns chilly and the leaves start to change my heart is happy. The fresh fruits and vegetables from autumn's harvest shine through in these cupcakes, from the cake to the frosting.

FOR CUPCAKES:

8 Medjool dates, pitted

5 eggs

½ cup (125 g) cooked sweet potato mash (about 1 small sweet potato)

⅓ cup (73 g) extra-virgin unrefined coconut oil, melted

2 teaspoons (10 ml) vanilla extract

½ cup (60 g) coconut flour

1½ teaspoons (3.5 g) ground cinnamon

1 teaspoon (1.8 g) ground ginger

½ teaspoon ground nutmeg

⅛ teaspoon ground cloves

½ teaspoon baking soda

½ teaspoon sea salt

½ cup (55 g) grated carrot

½ cup (55 g) grated apple

FOR PUMPKIN SPICED CREAM:

¾ cup (101 g) raw cashews, soaked in water for 3 hours at room temperature, water discarded

¼ cup (61 g) canned pumpkin purée

⅓ cup (80 ml) pure unsweetened apple juice

2 tablespoons (30 ml) canned coconut milk

2 Medjool dates, pitted

1 tablespoon (20 g) raw honey

¼ teaspoon pumpkin pie spice

Toasted pecans (optional, see Note, page 48)

Preheat the oven to 350°F (180°C, or gas mark 4). Line a 12-cup muffin pan with paper liners and set aside.

To make the cupcakes: In the bowl of a food processor, add the dates, eggs, sweet potato mash, coconut oil, and vanilla. Process until the dates are broken up and the mixture is smooth.

In a small bowl, whisk together the coconut flour, cinnamon, ginger, nutmeg, cloves, baking soda, and salt. Add the dry ingredients to the bowl of the food processor and process until smooth and everything is well combined. Remove the blade from the food processor, add the carrot and apple, and stir to incorporate.

Evenly distribute the batter among the prepared muffin liners. Bake the cupcakes for 25 to 30 minutes, or until golden and a toothpick inserted into the center of one comes out clean.

Allow the cupcakes to cool in the pan for 10 minutes before transferring to a wire rack to cool completely.

To make the cream: In the bowl of a food processor, combine the cashews, pumpkin purée, apple juice, coconut milk, dates, honey, and pumpkin pie spice and process until smooth. Refrigerate for 30 to 60 minutes, until chilled and thick enough to spread on the cupcakes. Spread the cream on the cooled cupcakes and top with the toasted pecans.

The cupcakes can be stored in an airtight container in the refrigerator for up to 4 days. Allow the cupcakes to come to room temperature before serving.

MAKES 12 CUPCAKES

Apple Spiced Cupcakes with "Caramel" Frosting

These cupcakes are moist and fragrant with fall's favorite spices. They remind me of caramel-dipped apples, but in cupcake form.

||||||||||||||||||||||||||||||||||||||||||||||||||||||||||||||||||||||||||||||||||||||

FOR CUPCAKES:

7 Medjool dates, pitted

4 eggs

⅔ cup (162 g) unsweetened applesauce

½ cup (109 g) extra-virgin unrefined coconut oil, melted

½ cup (120 ml) canned coconut milk

1½ teaspoons (7.5 ml) vanilla extract

3 cups (360 g) almond flour

3 tablespoons (24 g) coconut flour

1 teaspoon (4.6 g) baking soda

½ teaspoon unflavored gelatin

½ teaspoon sea salt

1 tablespoon (7 g) ground cinnamon

1 teaspoon (1.8 g) ground ginger

¼ teaspoon ground allspice

¼ teaspoon ground nutmeg

1½ cups (165 g) shredded apple

FOR "CARAMEL" FROSTING:

2 cups (350 g) Medjool dates, pitted and soaked in water to cover at room temperature for at least 4 hours

¼ cup (65 g) almond butter

1 tablespoon (15 ml) fresh lemon juice

½ teaspoon ground cinnamon

½ teaspoon sea salt

1 vanilla bean, split lengthwise, seeds scraped, and pod discarded (or 1 teaspoon vanilla extract)

Preheat the oven to 350°F (180°C, or gas mark 4) and line two 12-cup muffin pans with paper liners. Set aside.

To make the cupcakes: In the bowl of a food processor, add the dates, eggs, applesauce, coconut oil, coconut milk, and vanilla and process until the dates have completely broken up and are incorporated evenly into the batter.

In a small bowl, whisk together the almond flour, coconut flour, baking soda, gelatin, salt, cinnamon, ginger, allspice, and nutmeg. Add the dry ingredients to the wet ingredients and process until incorporated. Remove the blade from the food processor and stir in the apple.

Scoop the batter into the prepared pans, filling the cups to the rim. Bake for 30 to 35 minutes, or until the tops are golden and a toothpick inserted into the center of one comes out clean. Allow the cupcakes to cool for 10 minutes in the pan before transferring them to a wire rack to cool completely.

To make the frosting: Drain the dates and reserve the water. Add the dates to a food processor along with the almond butter, lemon juice, cinnamon, salt, and vanilla bean seeds. Blend on high until the dates are smooth. Add the soaking water, 1 tablespoon (15 ml) at a time, until the desired frosting consistency is reached.

Pipe the frosting onto the cupcakes using a pastry bag, or spread it with a spoon. Serve immediately.

The cupcakes can be stored in an airtight container in the refrigerator for up to 4 days. Allow the cupcakes to come to room temperature before serving.

MAKES 24 CUPCAKES

Maple Spiced Sweet Potato Cupcakes with Vanilla Cream

I adore sweet potatoes, especially in the fall. They bring a natural sweetness to any dish in an instant. An interesting fact on these beta-carotene–packed gems: sweet potatoes are *not* potatoes; they don't even come from the same plant family! They are, in fact, roots, compared to regular potatoes, which are tubers. Not in the mood for a cupcake? These can quickly be enjoyed as a morning muffin, minus the vanilla cream.

FOR CUPCAKES:

7 Medjool dates, pitted

¾ cup (184 g) cooked sweet potato mash (about 1 small sweet potato)

5 eggs, at room temperature

⅓ cup (73 g) extra-virgin unrefined coconut oil, melted

2 tablespoons (30 ml) canned coconut milk

2 teaspoons (10 ml) maple syrup

1 teaspoon (5 ml) vanilla extract

½ cup (60 g) coconut flour

1 tablespoon (7 g) ground cinnamon

½ teaspoon ground ginger

½ teaspoon baking soda

½ teaspoon sea salt

FOR VANILLA CREAM:

1 cup (135 g) raw cashews, soaked in water at room temperature for 3 hours, water discarded

½ cup (120 ml) canned coconut milk

2 Medjool dates, pitted

1 tablespoon (15 ml) maple syrup

1 vanilla bean, split lengthwise, seeds scraped, and pod discarded

FOR TOPPING:

½ cup (55 g) chopped pecans, toasted (optional, see Note, page 48)

Preheat the oven to 350°F (180°C, or gas mark 4) and line two 12-cup muffin pans with paper liners. Set aside.

To make the cupcakes: In the bowl of a food processor, add the dates, sweet potato mash, eggs, coconut oil, coconut milk, maple syrup, and vanilla extract and process until smooth and the dates are completely broken up.

In a small bowl, whisk together the coconut flour, cinnamon, ginger, baking soda, and salt.

Add the dry ingredients to the wet ingredients, process until fully incorporated.

Remove the blade from the bowl. Using an ice cream scoop, scoop batter evenly into the prepared muffin pans.

Bake for 30 to 40 minutes, or until a toothpick inserted in the middle of one comes out clean. Cool for 10 minutes before transferring to a wire rack to cool completely.

To make the Vanilla Cream: In the bowl of a food processor, combine the cashews, coconut milk, dates, maple syrup, and vanilla seeds and process until smooth. Refrigerator for 30 to 60 minutes, allowing to chill and thicken slightly.

Spread the cream on the cupcakes and top with toasted pecans, if using.

Cupcakes can be stored in an airtight container for up to 3 days in the refrigerator.

MAKES 24 CUPCAKES

Pumpkin Trifle

Although seemingly elaborate, trifles are quick to assemble. They make the perfect dessert to prepare a day ahead of a party or an event. That way, you will have one thing checked off your to-do list on the big day. In this trifle, the pumpkin layer is almost like a pumpkin pudding sweetened by a touch of maple syrup and banana.

2 cans (13½ ounces, or 400 g each) coconut milk, chilled overnight

1 can (15 ounces, or 420 g) pumpkin purée, chilled

½ cup (112 g) mashed ripe banana

1 tablespoon (15 ml) maple syrup, divided

1 teaspoon (5 ml) vanilla extract, divided

1 teaspoon (2.3 g) pumpkin pie spice

1 cup (40 g) crumbled Pumpkin Spiced Cookie Cutter Cookies (page 108)

For the pumpkin layer, take 1 can (13½ ounces, or 400 g) of the coconut milk and, being careful not to shake it, open it and remove the coconut cream that has settled at the top of the can. Add the coconut cream to a bowl along with the pumpkin purée, banana, ½ tablespoon (7.5 ml) of the maple syrup, ½ teaspoon of the vanilla, and pumpkin pie spice. Using a hand mixer, mix the ingredients to fully incorporate everything. Do not overmix.

Cover the pumpkin mixture with plastic wrap and refrigerate for at least 1 hour or overnight.

For the whipped layer, take the remaining 1 can (13½ ounces, or 400 g) coconut milk and again remove the top layer of coconut cream from the top of the can. Add the cream to a small bowl along with remaining ½ tablespoon (7.5 ml) maple syrup and remaining ½ teaspoon vanilla. Using a hand mixer, whip until peaks form, about 1 minute.

When ready to assemble, add a layer of cookie crumbs to the bottom of each of 4 dessert glasses. Top with a layer of the pumpkin mixture and then top with a layer of the whipped cream. Continue with one more layer of cookie crumbs, pumpkin, and whipped cream. Sprinkle the top of the trifle with additional cookie crumbs.

MAKES 4 TRIFLES

Apple-Walnut Cake

This extremely versatile cake can be dressed up or down depending on the occasion.
I have served this cake for brunch baked in a square dish, and I have served it at Thanksgiving.
You can't go wrong with the combination of sweet apples, cinnamon, and
the nutty flavor of the walnuts.

FOR CAKE:

3 cups (360 g) almond flour

½ teaspoon sea salt

1 teaspoon (4.6 g) baking soda

1 teaspoon (2.3 g) ground cinnamon

½ teaspoon ground ginger

¼ teaspoon nutmeg

½ cup (125 g) unsweetened applesauce

¼ cup (55 ml) extra-virgin unrefined coconut oil, melted

4 Medjool dates, pitted

3 eggs

1 tablespoon (15 ml) maple syrup

1 cup (110 g) shredded apple (about 1 small apple)

FOR TOPPING:

½ cup (72 g) chopped walnuts

2 teaspoons (10 ml) maple syrup

1½ teaspoons (7 g) extra-virgin unrefined coconut oil, melted

1 teaspoon (2.3 g) ground cinnamon

Pinch of sea salt

Preheat the oven to 350°F (180°C, or gas mark 4). Grease a 9-inch (23 cm) round cake pan with coconut oil.

To make the cake: In a small bowl, whisk together the almond flour, salt, baking soda, cinnamon, ginger, and nutmeg.

In the bowl of a food processor, add the applesauce, coconut oil, dates, eggs, and maple syrup. Process until the dates are completely broken up and the mixture is smooth. Add the dry ingredients to the bowl of the food processor and process until well combined. Remove the blade and stir in the apple. Pour the mixture into the prepared cake pan, spreading evenly.

To make the topping: In a small bowl, mix together the walnuts, maple syrup, coconut oil, cinnamon, and salt.

Spoon the topping over the cake evenly. Bake for 20 to 25 minutes, or until the cake is lightly golden and a toothpick inserted into the center comes out clean.

Let the cake cool in the pan for 15 minutes. Place a plate on top of the cake and then invert the cake onto the plate to unmold. Carefully turn the cake back over so the top is facing upward and transfer to a wire rack to cool completely.

Once cooled, slice and serve. The cake can be served alone or with some fresh coconut whipped cream (page 67).

The cake can be stored in an airtight container in the refrigerator for up to 4 days.

MAKES ONE 9-INCH (23 CM) CAKE

Coconut Sweet Potato Pumpkin Pie with Graham Cracker Crust

This is a twist on my grandmother's sweet potato pie that always graced the holiday table. This version is a mix between a sweet potato pie and a pumpkin pie and has minimal sweetener, allowing the sweet potato and pumpkin to really shine.

FOR GRAHAM CRACKER CRUST:

1½ cups (173 g) grain-free Graham Cracker crumbs (about 20 crackers, page 160)

3 tablespoons (41 g) ghee or coconut oil, melted

FOR FILLING:

5 dates, pitted

1¾ cups (430 g) cooked sweet potato mash (about 1 medium sweet potato)

¾ cup (184 g) pumpkin purée

3 eggs

½ cup (120 ml) canned coconut milk

1 tablespoon (15 ml) maple syrup

1 teaspoon (2.3 g) ground cinnamon

½ teaspoon ground ginger

¼ teaspoon ground cloves

¼ teaspoon sea salt

1 cup (80 g) unsweetened shredded coconut, lightly toasted, divided (see Note, page 31)

Preheat the oven to 350°F (180°C, or gas mark 4).

To make the crust: Place the graham cracker crumbs in a bowl and stir in the melted ghee to combine. Press the mixture into the bottom of a 9-inch (23 cm) glass pie plate, pressing evenly on the bottom and up the sides of the dish. Bake the crust for 5 minutes, and then allow to cool.

To make the filling: Place the dates in a heat-proof bowl. Add boiling water just to cover the dates. Allow the dates to sit in the water for 5 or 10 minutes, until soft. Drain some of the water, leaving about 1 tablespoon (15 ml), then use a fork to mash the dates until smooth.

Combine the date mash, sweet potato mash, pumpkin purée, eggs, coconut milk, maple syrup, cinnamon, ginger, cloves, and sea salt in the bowl of a food processor and process until smooth.

To prepare the pie, evenly sprinkle ½ cup (40 g) toasted coconut on the bottom section of the pie crust. Pour the pie filling over the coconut. Sprinkle the remaining ½ cup (40 g) coconut on top of the filling.

Transfer the pie to a baking sheet and then place a pie shield around the pie, to ensure the crust doesn't burn, and bake for 50 to 60 minutes, or until the filling has set. If you don't have a pie shield, you can form a protective layer around the edge of the crust with aluminum foil.

The pie keeps best covered and stored in the refrigerator for up to 4 days.

MAKES ONE 9-INCH (23 CM) PIE

Butternut Squash Cinnamon Almond Tart

Roasted butternut squash makes a nice change from pumpkin for your Thanksgiving or autumn dessert. The pairing of the nutty, sweet flavor of almonds and the spice of cinnamon makes this rustic-style tart a comforting dish on cooler autumn days. Take it up a notch and serve with coconut whipped cream (page 138) or Vanilla Coconut Ice Cream (page 141). And if you prefer, you can also shape this tart into a square.

||||||||||||||||||||||||||||||||||||||||||||||||||||||||||||||||||||||||||||||||||||||||||||||||||||||||||||||||||||||||||

FOR CRUST:

1½ cups (180 g) almond flour

1 cup (80 g) unsweetened shredded coconut

½ teaspoon ground cinnamon

¼ teaspoon sea salt

¼ cup (56 g) extra-virgin unrefined coconut oil (no need to melt)

2 egg yolks

1 tablespoon (15 ml) maple syrup

FOR FILLING:

1 medium butternut squash, peeled, halved, seeded, and cut into ½-inch (1.3 cm) slices

2 teaspoons (4.7 g) extra-virgin unrefined coconut oil, melted

¼ cup (60 ml) maple syrup, divided

1 teaspoon (2.3 g) ground cinnamon, divided

¼ teaspoon plus a pinch of sea salt, divided

½ cup (55 g) sliced almonds, toasted (see Note, page 48) and ground

1 teaspoon (2.5 g) coconut flour

1 egg

½ teaspoon vanilla extract

1 tablespoon (7 g) sliced almonds, toasted (see Note, page 48)

Preheat the oven to 450°F (230°C, or gas mark 8).

To make the crust: In the bowl of a food processor, add the almond flour, coconut, cinnamon, and salt and pulse 4 or 5 times until a fine meal forms. Add the coconut oil, egg yolks, and maple syrup and process again until a ball of dough forms. If the dough is still crumbly, add 1 tablespoon (15 ml) water or coconut milk until the dough forms a ball. Remove the dough, wrap in plastic wrap, and refrigerate for 1 hour.

To make the filling: On a rimmed baking sheet, toss the butternut squash with the coconut oil, 1 tablespoon (15 ml) of the maple syrup, ½ teaspoon of the cinnamon, and a pinch of sea salt. Roast until golden and tender, 15 to 20 minutes.

Remove from the oven and lower heat to 350°F (180°C, or gas mark 4).

In a small bowl, stir together the remaining 3 tablespoon (45 ml) maple syrup, remaining ½ teaspoon cinnamon, the ground almonds, coconut flour, egg, vanilla extract, and remaining ¼ teaspoon salt.

Remove the ball of dough from the refrigerator and place on a sheet of parchment paper. Dust the top of the ball with a little coconut flour or almond flour and place another piece of parchment paper, even in size, on top of the dough. Using a rolling pin, roll the dough into a circle or an oval about ½ inch (1.3 cm) thick. Remove the top layer of parchment paper and transfer the bottom piece of parchment with the dough onto a rimmed baking sheet. Spread the almond mixture on top, leaving a 2-inch (5 cm) margin around the edges. Top with the roasted squash. Carefully fold the dough over on each side, along the 2-inch (5 cm) margins, toward the center. Refrigerate for about 30 minutes, until firm.

Bake the tart until the crust is golden brown, 30 to 35 minutes.

Remove from the oven and allow to cool. Sprinkle with toasted sliced almonds. Cut and serve.

Store in an airtight container in refrigerator for up to 3 days.

MAKES 8 SERVINGS

Butternut Squash Apple Hazelnut Mini Cakes

Remarkably moist and tender, these cakes get warmth from the cinnamon, cloves, and ginger. The almond flour and hazelnut meal add nutrients without compromising taste or texture. These mini cakes can also be transformed easily into an 8-inch (20 cm) cake. Either way, these autumn flavors will be a winner.

½ **small butternut squash, peeled, seeded, and diced**

3 eggs

7 Medjool dates, pitted

⅓ **cup (80 ml) canned coconut milk**

3 tablespoons (41 g) extra-virgin unrefined coconut oil, melted

1 teaspoon (5 ml) vanilla extract

1 cup (120 ml) almond flour

⅓ **cup (40 g) hazelnut meal**

1 teaspoon (2.3 g) ground cinnamon

½ **teaspoon ground ginger**

¼ **teaspoon ground cloves**

½ **teaspoon baking soda**

½ **teaspoon sea salt**

1 Gala or Fuji apple, peeled, cored, and finely diced

1 ounce (28 g) hazelnuts, chopped

Preheat the oven to 350°F (180°C, or gas mark 4). Grease a 12-cup muffin pan with coconut oil and set aside.

Steam the diced squash until tender, about 10 minutes depending on the size of dice. Purée in a food processor and measure out ¾ cup (184 g). Reserve the remaining butternut squash for another use.

In the bowl of a food processor, combine the butternut squash, eggs, dates, coconut milk, coconut oil, and vanilla and process until completely combined and the dates are broken up.

In a medium bowl, whisk together the almond flour, hazelnut meal, cinnamon, ginger, cloves, baking soda, and salt. Pour the dry ingredients into the wet ingredients and process again until well incorporated.

Remove the blade from the food processor and fold in the apple.

Pour the batter evenly among the muffin cups and sprinkle the tops with the hazelnuts. Bake for 20 to 25 minutes, or until golden and a toothpick inserted into the center of one comes out clean.

Cool in the pan for 10 minutes before transferring to a wire rack to cool completely.

The cakes can be stored in an airtight container in the refrigerator for up to 4 days. Bring to room temperature before serving.

MAKES 12 MINI CAKES

Pumpkin Ginger Ice Cream Tartlets

These simple tarts are easy to make and have only a short list of ingredients.
You can play around with the pumpkin, too, and swap it out with sweet potato
purée or even a ripe banana for a year-round option.

4 or 5 Graham Crackers (page 160)

⅓ cup (82 g) pumpkin purée

2 tablespoons (30 ml) maple syrup

2 teaspoons (4 g) peeled and grated fresh ginger

1 can (13½ ounces, or 400 ml) coconut milk, refrigerated overnight

Line 6 cups of a muffin tin with liners. Break the cookies into coarse crumbs and divide among the paper liners, reserving about 1 table-spoon (7 g) for sprinkling. Make sure the crumb base is level.

In a small bowl, combine the pumpkin, maple syrup, and ginger.

Remove the coconut milk from the refrigerator, being careful not to shake it. Open the can and carefully remove the solid cream that has formed at the top of the can. Place in a bowl and, using a hand mixer, whip the coconut cream until you have soft peaks. Add the pumpkin mixture and continue to mix for another minute or so to thicken it up.

Divide the mixture among the prepared cups. Sprinkle with the reserved crumbs. Freeze for at least 6 hours before serving.

To serve, remove from the paper liner and thaw for 10 minutes.

The tartlets can be stored in an airtight container in the freezer for up to 2 weeks.

MAKES 6 TARTLETS

Acorn Squash Bars

Sweet, nutty acorn squash is an appealing alternative to pumpkin or butternut squash during the autumn months. Acorn squash is a great source of antioxidants and is also an anti-inflammatory food.

||||||||||||||||||||||||||||||||||||||||||||||||||||||||||||||||||||||||||||||||||||||||||||||||

6 eggs

5 Medjool dates, pitted

½ cup (125 g) acorn squash purée (see Note)

⅓ cup (73 ml) extra-virgin unrefined coconut oil, melted

¼ cup (60 ml) canned coconut milk

2 tablespoons (30 ml) maple syrup

1 teaspoon (5 ml) vanilla extract

½ cup (60 g) coconut flour

1 teaspoon (2.3 g) ground cinnamon

½ teaspoon ground ginger

½ teaspoon baking soda

½ teaspoon unflavored gelatin

¼ teaspoon sea salt

Preheat the oven to 350°F (180°C, or gas mark 4) and grease an 8 x 8-inch (20 x 20 cm) baking pan with coconut oil. Be sure to grease really well to avoid the cake sticking to the pan.

In the bowl of a food processor, combine the eggs, dates, squash purée, coconut oil, coconut milk, maple syrup, and vanilla and process until smooth and the dates are completely broken up.

In a small bowl, whisk together the coconut flour, cinnamon, ginger, baking soda, gelatin, and salt. Add the dry ingredients to the bowl of the food processor and process again until fully incorporated.

Pour the batter into the prepared dish. Bake for 30 to 35 minutes, or until a toothpick inserted into the center of the cake comes out clean. Allow to cool on a wire rack before cutting into sixteen 2-inch (5 cm) bars and serving.

The bars are best stored in an airtight container in the refrigerator for up to 3 days. Reheat to serve.

MAKES 16 BARS

Note: To make acorn squash purée, preheat the oven to 400°F (200°C, or gas mark 6). Cut the acorn squash in half and remove the interior seeds and stringy membranes. Place the halves, flesh side down, on a baking sheet and bake for 20 to 25 minutes. Turn the squash, flesh side up, and bake for an additional 25 minutes, until the flesh is tender and soft.

Baked Crumble-Stuffed Apples

I like using Granny Smith, Honey Crisp, or Fuji apples for this recipe, but use your area's favorite apple. I cored the apples for a lighter filling, but if you want more filling, scoop out the inside of your apple a little more.

‖‖

8 apples, cored

½ lemon

½ cup (60 g) almond flour

¼ cup (34 g) chopped pecans, lightly toasted (see Note, page 48)

¼ cup (34 g) chopped walnuts, lightly toasted (see Note, page 48)

4 Medjool dates, pitted and chopped

1 teaspoon (2.3 g) ground cinnamon

½ teaspoon ground ginger

¼ teaspoon ground nutmeg

¼ teaspoon ground cloves

¼ teaspoon sea salt

3 tablespoons (41 g) extra-virgin unrefined coconut oil, melted

1 tablespoon (15 ml) maple syrup

Preheat the oven to 350°F (180°C, or gas mark 4). Line a baking dish large enough for the apples with parchment paper. Squeeze the lemon half's juice over the apples.

In a small bowl, whisk together the almond flour, pecans, walnuts, dates, cinnamon, ginger, nutmeg, cloves, and salt. Add the coconut oil and maple syrup and stir until the mixture becomes slightly wet.

Carefully stuff the centers of the apples with the mixture, and place the apples in the prepared baking dish.

Cover the apples loosely with aluminum foil, and bake for 40 to 45 minutes, or until softened.

Allow the apples to cool for 10 minutes before serving. Serve with an optional scoop of Vanilla Coconut Ice Cream (page 141).

These are best served and enjoyed immediately after baking.

MAKES 8 SERVINGS

Carrot-Apple Whoopie Pies

These melt-in-your-mouth whoopie pies remind me of the soft oatmeal pies
I had as a child, but of course without all the sugar.

FOR CAKES:

3 Medjool dates, pitted

1 egg

¼ cup (60 g) unsweetened applesauce

¼ cup (55 g) extra-virgin unrefined coconut oil, melted

1 tablespoon (15 ml) maple syrup

2 teaspoons (10 ml) vanilla extract

1½ cups (180 g) almond flour

2 tablespoons (14 g) coconut flour

1 teaspoon (2.3 g) ground cinnamon

½ teaspoon ground ginger

½ teaspoon baking soda

¼ teaspoon sea salt

½ cup (55 g) grated carrot

⅓ cup (37 g) grated apple

FOR FILLING:

1 cup (135 g) raw cashews, soaked in water overnight at room temperature

½ cup (120 ml) pure unsweetened apple juice

¼ teaspoon ground cinnamon

¼ teaspoon ground ginger

1 tablespoon (15 ml) maple syrup

2 Medjool dates, pitted

½ teaspoon vanilla extract

Preheat the oven to 350°F (180°C, or gas mark 4). Line a baking sheet with parchment paper.

To make the cakes: In the bowl of a food processor, add the dates, egg, applesauce, coconut oil, maple syrup, and vanilla and process until smooth and the dates are completely broken up. Add the almond flour, coconut flour, cinnamon, ginger, baking soda, and salt and process again to combine everything. Remove the blade from the food processor and stir in the carrot and apple.

Using an ice cream scoop, scoop the batter onto the prepared baking sheet, making 12 cookies and spacing the cookies about 1 inch (2.5 cm) apart. Bake for 20 to 25 minutes, or until the cookies are golden. Allow the cookies to cool 10 to 15 minutes before transferring them to a wire rack to cool completely.

To make the filling: Drain the cashews and add them to the bowl of a food processor along with the apple juice, cinnamon, ginger, maple syrup, dates, and vanilla. Process until completely smooth, stopping a couple of times to scrape down the sides of the bowl. Refrigerate the mixture for 30 minutes.

To assemble the whoopie pies, turn half of the cookies face down (so the flat sides are facing up). Scoop about 1 tablespoon (14 g) filling onto the center of each. Place the remaining cookies with the bottom (flat side) facing down on top of the filling and slightly press together.

Store whoopie pies in an airtight container in the refrigerator up to 4 days. Whoopie pies can also be frozen, but allow them to come to room temperature before enjoying.

MAKES 6 WHOOPIE PIES

Maple Cinnamon Pecan Pie

Pecan pie is one of my husband's all-time favorite holiday desserts, so it was a "must" to turn Paleo. This version received a thumbs-up from my husband, and best of all, it doesn't use the many cups of sugar and corn syrup of the traditional version. A winner for everyone!

FOR CRUST:

1½ cups (180 g) almond flour

½ cup (60 g) hazelnut flour

¼ cup (30 g) coconut flour

½ teaspoon ground cinnamon

½ teaspoon unflavored gelatin

¼ teaspoon sea salt

2 Medjool dates, pitted

⅓ cup (73 g) extra-virgin unrefined coconut oil, melted

1 tablespoon (20 g) raw honey

FOR FILLING:

3 Medjool dates, pitted

4 eggs

½ cup (120 ml) maple syrup

2 tablespoons (27 g) extra-virgin unrefined coconut oil, melted

1 tablespoon (15 ml) vanilla extract

2 teaspoons (4.6 g) ground cinnamon

1½ cups (202 g) pecan halves

Preheat the oven to 350°F (180°C, or gas mark 4).

To make the crust: Place the almond flour, hazelnut flour, coconut flour, cinnamon, gelatin, and salt in the bowl of a food processor and pulse to combine. Add the dates, coconut oil, and honey and process again until a dough forms. Press the dough onto the bottom and up the sides of a 9-inch (23 cm) pie plate. Refrigerate for 30 minutes.

To make the filling: Place the dates in a heat-proof bowl. Add boiling water just to cover the dates. Allow the dates to sit in the water for 5 or 10 minutes, until soft. Drain some of the water, leaving about 1 tablespoon (15 ml), then use a fork to mash the dates until smooth.

In the bowl of a food processor or blender, combine the date mash, eggs, maple syrup, coconut oil, vanilla, and cinnamon and process until smooth.

Remove the pie crust from the refrigerator and set on a baking sheet. Pour in the filling and arrange the pecan halves on top. Cover the edges of the pie with a pie shield or aluminum foil to prevent burning. Bake for about 40 minutes. The center should still be a little wobbly. Allow to cool completely before serving with Vanilla Coconut Ice Cream (page 141).

The pie is best kept covered in the refrigerator for up to 4 days. It can also be frozen, well covered, for up to 45 days.

MAKES ONE 9-INCH (23 CM) PIE

Pumpkin Spiced Bundt Cake

Pumpkin is one of the great treasures of fall. The smaller sugar pumpkins are the sweetest and have a close-grained flesh, which makes them perfect for making your own pumpkin purée. Making purée and freezing it is a great way you can enjoy your favorite pumpkin treats, such as this Bundt cake, into winter.

1 cup (245 g) pumpkin purée

6 Medjool dates, pitted

6 eggs

½ cup (120 ml) canned coconut milk

⅓ cup (73 g) extra-virgin unrefined coconut oil, melted

1 teaspoon (2.3 ml) vanilla extract

1 cup (120 g) almond flour

½ cup (60 g) coconut flour

1 teaspoon (4.6 g) baking soda

1½ teaspoons (3.5 g) ground cinnamon

½ teaspoon ground ginger

¼ teaspoon ground cloves

¼ teaspoons ground nutmeg

¼ teaspoon sea salt

Preheat the oven to 350°F (180°C, or gas mark 4). Grease an 8- or 9-inch (20 or 23 cm) Bundt cake pan with coconut oil.

In the bowl of a food processor, add the pumpkin purée, dates, eggs, coconut milk, coconut oil, and vanilla and process until smooth and the dates are broken up.

In a small bowl, whisk together the almond flour, coconut flour, baking soda, cinnamon, ginger, cloves, nutmeg, and salt. Add the dry ingredients to the wet ingredients and process until well incorporated.

Pour the batter into the prepared cake pan and bake for 35 to 40 minutes, or until a toothpick inserted near the center comes out clean.

Allow the cake to cool in the pan for 10 to 15 minutes before releasing from the pan to cool completely.

Cover the cake and store in the refrigerator or in a cool place for up to 3 days.

MAKES ONE 8- OR 9-INCH (20 OR 23 CM) CAKE

Pumpkin Spiced Cookie Cutter Cookies

These are fun cookies to make with kids around Halloween or even Thanksgiving. The kids will love cutting out the pumpkin shapes, and they will anticipate tasting their finished creations. These do need time to sit in the refrigerator, so don't skip that step, or the cookies will be a bit hard to work with. If you are short on time, place in the freezer for half the time stated for the refrigerator.

2 cups (240 g) almond flour

1 teaspoon (4.6 g) baking soda

1 teaspoon (2.3 g) unflavored gelatin

1 teaspoon (2.3 g) ground cinnamon

½ teaspoon ground ginger

⅛ teaspoon ground nutmeg

⅛ teaspoon ground cloves

Pinch of sea salt

2 tablespoons (27 g) extra-virgin unrefined coconut oil, melted

2 tablespoons (30 ml) maple syrup

2 tablespoons (30 g) pumpkin purée

1 tablespoon (15 ml) canned coconut milk

1 teaspoon (5 ml) vanilla extract

Preheat the oven to 350°F (180°C, or gas mark 4). Line a baking sheet with parchment paper and set aside.

In the bowl of a food processor, add the almond flour, baking soda, gelatin, cinnamon, ginger, nutmeg, cloves, and salt and pulse to combine.

Add the coconut oil, maple syrup, pumpkin purée, coconut milk, and vanilla to the bowl and process until a ball of dough forms. Wrap the dough with plastic wrap and refrigerate for 1 hour.

Dust the dough with almond flour and roll to ¼-inch (6 mm) thick between two pieces of parchment paper. Using the cookie cutter of your choice, cut out cookies and carefully place the cutouts on the prepared baking sheet. Re-roll the dough and cut out more cookies. You should get 12.

Bake the cookies for 10 to 12 minutes, or until just golden around the edges.

Allow the cookies to cool for 5 to 10 minutes on the pan before transferring them to a wire rack to cool completely.

The cookies are best if stored in an airtight container for up to 4 days. Cookies can also be frozen and enjoyed at a later time.

MAKES 12 COOKIES

chapter six

WINTER INDULGENCES:
GOODIES TO WARM YOU UP WHEN IT'S COLD OUTSIDE

As each year comes to an end, a new season arrives—and with it a supply of fresh ingredients that offer you comfort from the cold temperatures outside. Winter produce delivers a surprising range of flavors for you to enjoy with family and friends. Let the dessert recipes of this chapter warm your soul with tangy cranberries, tart pomegranate, vibrant citrus fruits, and uniquely sweet kiwi.

• **Cranberries:** These berries are glossy, scarlet red, and very tart. Fresh cranberries, which contain the highest levels of beneficial nutrients, are at their peak from October through early January, just in time to add their festive hue, tangy flavor, and numerous health-protective benefits to your holiday meals. Unlike any other fruit, cranberries need to be cooked to release their full flavor and to absorb that of other ingredients. When shopping, choose fresh, plump cranberries, deep red in color, and quite firm to the touch.

• **Pomegranates:** The pomegranate is a lovely fruit that is between a lemon and a grapefruit in size, and usually in a rounded shape with a thick reddish skin. They are packed with antioxidants equal to those in green tea and red wine, and are especially loaded with vitamin C and potassium. Although the membranes of pomegranates are bitter and inedible, the pulp and seeds contribute a juicy, sweet-tart flavor to many winter recipes. Choose pomegranates that feel heavy, are bright in color, and are free of blemishes. They are typically in season from September to February.

• **Oranges:** Oranges are one of the most popular fruits around the world. These round, finely textured fruits are often enjoyed in many fashions: sectioned, sliced, juiced, or zested—all of which make them the perfect fruit to add flavor to a dessert. Oranges are generally available from winter through summer, with seasonal variations depending on the variety, such as navels (winter), blood oranges, and clementines. Keep in mind when shopping for this great fruit that oranges that are partially green or have brown spots may be just as ripe and tasty as those that are solid orange in color. And, because oranges are among the top twenty foods in which pesticide residues are most frequently found, buy organic oranges whenever possible, especially when you are using the zest.

Cranberry-Apple Upside-Down Cakes

I love the combination of tart fresh cranberries with the sweetness of apples in these mini upside-down cakes. Cranberries are powerhouses in antioxidants and contain compounds that play an important role in protecting your body's cells from free-radical damage, actually more so than cranberry juice.

FOR CAKE:

7 Medjool dates, pitted

2 to 3 tablespoons (30 to 45 ml) boiling water, or more as needed

3 eggs

½ cup (125 g) unsweetened applesauce

½ cup (109 g) extra-virgin unrefined coconut oil, melted

¼ cup (60 ml) canned coconut milk

1½ teaspoons (7.5 ml) vanilla extract

2½ cups (300 g) almond flour

½ cup (60 g) hazelnut flour

¼ cup (30 g) coconut flour

1 teaspoon (4.6 g) baking soda

½ teaspoon sea salt

1 tablespoon (7 g) ground cinnamon

1 teaspoon (1.8 g) ground ginger

1½ cups (165 g) shredded apple

FOR APPLE-CRANBERRY LAYER:

1 cup (150 g) chopped apple

½ cup (50 g) fresh cranberries

1 tablespoon (6 g) orange zest

½ teaspoon ground cinnamon

½ teaspoon ground ginger

1½ tablespoons (30 g) raw honey

Preheat the oven to 350°F (180°C, or gas mark 4) and grease a 6-cup (large) muffin tin with coconut oil and lightly dust with coconut flour. Set aside.

To make the cake: Mash the dates by adding the boiling water, or enough boiling water to cover the dates, and allow them to sit in water for a few minutes. Drain some of the water, leaving about 1 tablespoon (15 ml), then use a fork to mash the dates until smooth.

In a large bowl using a hand mixer, mix together the mashed dates, eggs, applesauce, coconut oil, coconut milk, and vanilla.

In a medium bowl, whisk together the almond flour, hazelnut flour, coconut flour, baking soda, salt, cinnamon, and ginger. Add the dry ingredients to the wet ingredients and mix with the hand mixer until well combined. Stir in the apple.

To make the apple-cranberry layer: In a small bowl, toss together the apple, cranberries, orange zest, cinnamon, ginger, and honey. Arrange the mixture in a single layer on the bottom of each muffin cup. Top each evenly with the cake batter.

Bake for 30 to 35 minutes, or until golden brown and a toothpick inserted into the center of one comes out clean.

Allow the cakes to cool completely before gently turning over the pan to release the cakes.

The cakes can be kept in an airtight container in a cool, dry place for up to 3 days or in the refrigerator for up to 5 days.

MAKES 6 CAKES

Nutty Christmas Bark

If you are looking for the perfect gift for the holiday season, this may be the one. This recipe is versatile and can be changed to include whatever nuts or dried fruits you have in your pantry. I always try to customize it depending on which friend or family member I'm giving this special gift to.

1 cup (175 g) chopped dark chocolate (85% cacao or higher)

½ cup (55 g) blanched almond slices

⅓ cup (50 g) unsweetened dried cranberries

¼ cup (20 g) unsweetened shredded coconut

Line a rimmed baking sheet with parchment paper or waxed paper.

Prepare a double boiler by setting a glass bowl over a pot of simmering water, but do not let the bowl touch the water. Place the chocolate in the bowl of the double boiler and let sit until almost completely melted. Remove the bowl from the heat, stir the chocolate until smooth, then spread over the prepared baking sheet to your desired thickness. Sprinkle the almonds, cranberries, and coconut over the melted chocolate. Refrigerate until the chocolate is set, 20 to 30 minutes. Once set, break or cut into pieces.

The bark can be stored in an airtight container in the refrigerator for at least 1 week or in the freezer for 30 days.

MAKES TEN 1-OUNCE (28 G) SERVINGS

Cranberry Pear Tart

Pears bring a slight sweetness and earthy flavor to this tart and pair nicely with the tartness of the cranberries. Pears come in many varieties; have fun picking your favorite for this tart.

FOR CRUST:

1 cup (120 g) almond flour

½ cup (70 g) pecans, chopped

6 dates, pitted

¼ cup (55 g) extra-virgin unrefined coconut oil, melted

1 teaspoon (5 ml) vanilla extract

½ teaspoon ground cinnamon

½ teaspoon sea salt

¼ cup (20 g) unsweetened shredded coconut

FOR FILLING:

2 pears, cored and thinly sliced

2 cups (200 g) fresh cranberries

⅓ cup (80 ml) maple syrup

¼ cup (55 g) extra-virgin unrefined coconut oil, melted

1 teaspoon (5 ml) vanilla extract

½ teaspoon ground cinnamon

¼ teaspoon ground cardamom

¼ teaspoon ground ginger

¼ teaspoon sea salt

Zest of 1 lemon

1 egg, whisked

Preheat the oven to 350°F (180°C, or gas mark 4). Grease a 9-inch (23 cm) tart pan with coconut oil and set aside.

To make the crust: Combine the almond flour, pecans, dates, coconut oil, vanilla, cinnamon, salt, and coconut in a food processor and pulse until well mixed and the dates are broken up. Press the crust evenly along the bottom of the prepared pan.

To make the filling: Layer the pear slices on top of the crust; a bit of overlap is okay. In a large bowl, combine the cranberries, maple syrup, coconut oil, vanilla, cinnamon, cardamom, ginger, salt, and lemon zest and stir until well combined. Add the egg and stir to combine. Pour the filling on top of the crust and pear layer and spread evenly. Bake for 35 to 40 minutes, or until the crust is golden and the filling is just slightly set. Allow the tart to cool completely before removing from the tart pan.

Slice and serve with Vanilla Coconut Ice Cream (page 141), if desired.

The tart can be covered and stored in the refrigerator for up to 3 days. Warm before serving.

MAKES ONE 9-INCH (23 CM) TART

Maple Date Pecan Squares

The maple syrup gives these date pecan bars their distinctive flavor. Transform these squares from a simple snack to an indulgent dessert by adding a scoop of Vanilla Coconut Ice Cream (page 141) while they are still slightly warm.

FOR CRUST:

1½ cups (180 g) almond flour

2 tablespoons (30 ml) maple syrup

2 tablespoons (28 g) extra-virgin unrefined coconut oil (no need to melt)

1 teaspoon (2.3 g) ground cinnamon

½ teaspoon ground ginger

¼ teaspoon ground nutmeg

¼ teaspoon ground cloves

¼ teaspoon baking soda

¼ teaspoon sea salt

FOR FILLING:

6 tablespoons (84 g) extra-virgin unrefined coconut oil (no need to melt)

3 tablespoons (45 ml) maple syrup

⅓ cup (80 ml) canned coconut milk

7 Medjool dates, pitted and chopped

2 cups (270 g) pecans, coarsely chopped

1 teaspoon (2.3 g) ground cinnamon

Pinch of sea salt

Preheat the oven to 350°F (180°C, or gas mark 4). Line an 8 x 8-inch (20 x 20 cm) pan with parchment paper, allowing the paper to extend over the edges of the pan. This will help in removing the bars from the pan once baked.

To make the crust: In a small bowl, combine the almond flour, maple syrup, coconut oil, cinnamon, ginger, nutmeg, cloves, baking soda, and salt. Stir with a fork until a crust forms. Press the crust mixture into the prepared baking dish, forming an even layer across the bottom of the pan. Bake for 10 to 15 minutes, or until golden. Allow the crust to cool completely.

To make the filling: In a medium saucepan over medium heat, combine the coconut oil and maple syrup, stirring together until combined and smooth. Bring to a light boil, remove from the heat, and immediately stir in the coconut milk. Stir in the dates, pecans, cinnamon, and salt.

Pour the hot filling over the cooled crust, spreading it evenly to the edges with a spatula. Bake until the filling is set when you give the pan a gentle shake, 22 to 25 minutes. Let the bars cool on a wire rack before cutting into sixteen 2-inch (5 cm) squares.

The squares can be kept in an airtight container in the refrigerator for up to 4 days. The bars can also be frozen and then brought to room temperature before enjoying.

MAKES 16 SQUARES

Orange Pomegranate Cupcakes with Orange Cream

These subtly sweet cupcakes shine with the tastes of winter's favorite fruits: oranges and pomegranates. When I was growing up, pomegranates often graced my lunch box. The other kids would stare in wonderment as to what exactly I was eating. I'd sit with red hands and face and eat the pomegranate seed by seed. They are a fun fruit, and they're packed with great antioxidants that protect against heart disease and cancer.

FOR CUPCAKES:

8 eggs

2 Medjool dates, pitted

½ cup (109 g) extra-virgin unrefined coconut oil, melted

¼ cup (120 ml) freshly squeezed orange juice

¼ cup (60 ml) freshly squeezed pomegranate juice

¼ cup (60 ml) maple syrup

¼ cup (60 ml) canned coconut milk

2 teaspoons (3.5 g) orange zest

1½ teaspoons (7.5 ml) vanilla extract

1 cup (120 g) coconut flour

1 teaspoon (4.6 g) baking soda

½ teaspoon sea salt

FOR ORANGE CREAM:

2 cans (13½ ounces, or 400 ml each) coconut milk, refrigerated overnight

1½ teaspoons (10 g) raw honey

1 teaspoon (5 ml) freshly squeezed orange juice

1 teaspoon (5 ml) vanilla extract

¼ teaspoon sea salt

Orange zest

Pomegranate arils

Preheat the oven to 350°F (180°C, or gas mark 4). Line a 12-cup muffin pan with cupcake liners and set aside.

To make the cupcakes: In the bowl of a food processor, process the eggs, dates, coconut oil, orange juice, pomegranate juice, maple syrup, coconut milk, orange zest, and vanilla until smooth and the dates are completely broken up.

In a small bowl, whisk together the coconut flour, baking soda, and salt. Add the dry ingredients to the wet ingredients and process until fully incorporated.

Remove the blade from the food processor and carefully scoop the batter into the prepared muffin pan. Bake for 30 to 35 minutes, or until golden and a toothpick inserted into the center of one comes out clean. Cool the cupcakes completely.

To make the cream: Without shaking the cans, carefully remove the top layer of coconut cream from the canned coconut milk and place in a bowl with the honey, orange juice, vanilla, and salt. Use a hand mixer to whip until the cream starts to form peaks.

Using a pastry bag, pipe the cream onto the cooled cupcakes or use a knife to coat the tops of the cupcakes. Garnish with additional orange zest and pomegranate arils.

The cupcakes are best stored in an airtight container in the refrigerator for up to 3 days. Bring to room temperature before serving.

MAKES 12 CUPCAKES

Kiwi Pops

A kiwi is packed with more vitamin C than the equivalent amount of orange. These bright green–fleshed fruits speckled with tiny black seeds add a dramatic tropical flair to these easy pops.

---

3 kiwis

½ cup (88 g) chopped 100% cacao dark chocolate

2 tablespoons (28 g) extra-virgin unrefined coconut oil (no need to melt)

2 teaspoons (14 g) raw honey

¼ cup (20 g) unsweetened shredded coconut

Peel and slice each kiwi into four rounds ½- to 1-inch (1.3 to 2.5 cm) thick.

Carefully pierce the center of each kiwi slice with a wooden or lollipop stick and set on a baking sheet or plate lined with waxed paper. Once all the kiwi slices are on the sticks, transfer to the freezer and freeze for at least 10 hours, or overnight.

Once the kiwis are frozen, prepare a double boiler by setting a glass bowl over a pot of simmering water, but do not let the bowl touch the water. Melt the chocolate, coconut oil, and honey in the double boiler, stirring constantly until smooth and melted.

Carefully dip the kiwi pops into the chocolate to completely cover the kiwi, and then immediately sprinkle with the shredded coconut. Transfer to a clean sheet of waxed paper. Finish the remaining pops and transfer to the freezer to allow the chocolate to set.

Keep the pops in an airtight container in the freezer until ready to serve or up to 7 days.

MAKES 12 POPS

Honey Spiced Orange Cake

The most important aspect of this simple cake is the orange flavor that shines throughout. Adding fresh orange juice, orange zest, and a sweetened honey-orange syrup allows this cake to speak volumes. Transform this cake into a bread by simply using a bread pan instead.

FOR CAKE:

2¼ cups (270 g) almond flour

1 teaspoon (2.3 g) ground cinnamon

¾ teaspoon baking soda

½ teaspoon ground ginger

¼ teaspoon ground nutmeg

¼ teaspoon sea salt

¼ cup (55 ml) extra-virgin unrefined coconut oil, melted

4 Medjool dates, pitted

3 eggs

¼ cup (60 ml) freshly squeezed orange juice

1 tablespoon (20 g) raw honey

2 teaspoons (3.6 g) orange zest

FOR HONEY-ORANGE SYRUP:

¼ cup (60 ml) freshly squeezed orange juice

1 tablespoon (20 g) raw honey

Preheat the oven to 350°F (180°C, or gas mark 4). Grease a 9-inch (23 cm) round cake pan with coconut oil.

To make the cake: In a small bowl, whisk together the almond flour, cinnamon, baking soda, ginger, nutmeg, and salt.

In the bowl of a food processor, process the coconut oil, dates, eggs, orange juice, honey, and orange zest until the dates are completely broken up and the mixture is smooth. Add the dry ingredients to the wet and process until well combined.

Pour the mixture into the prepared cake pan, spreading evenly. Bake for 20 to 25 minutes, or until lightly golden and a toothpick inserted into the center comes out clean.

Let the cake cool in the pan for 15 minutes.

Meanwhile, to make the syrup: In a small saucepan over medium heat, combine the orange juice and honey and stir until the honey is completely dissolved. Once dissolved, continue to cook for 2 more minutes while stirring constantly. Remove from the heat and allow to cool for 5 minutes.

Line a baking sheet with parchment paper and invert the cake onto it. Use a toothpick to poke holes in the top of the cake.

Brush the top of the cake with the honey-orange syrup and allow the syrup to soak into the cake. Let the cake cool completely, at least 30 minutes.

Once cooled, slice and serve with coconut whipped cream (page 67) and dust with orange zest.

The cake is best stored in an airtight container or wrapped in plastic wrap and placed in the refrigerator for up to 4 days.

MAKES ONE 9-INCH (23 CM) CAKE

Molten Orange-Chocolate Lava Cakes

This dessert of rich, dark chocolate cake surrounding a molten core of orange-spiced chocolate will leave your dinner guests speechless. It is the perfect option for an after-dinner dessert. You can prep it the day before and pop it in the oven just 10 minutes before you are ready to serve.

||||||||||||||||||||||||||||||||||||||||||||||||||||||||||||||||||||||||||||||||||||||||||||||||||||||||||||||||||||||||||||||||||

6 tablespoons (84 g) extra-virgin unrefined coconut oil

3 ounces (42 g) dark chocolate (85% cacao or higher), chopped

4 ounces (56 g) unsweetened dark chocolate, chopped

¼ cup (80 g) raw honey

1 tablespoon (6 g) orange zest, plus extra for garnishing

1½ teaspoons (7.5 ml) freshly squeezed orange juice

1 teaspoon (5 ml) vanilla extract

3 tablespoons (24 g) almond flour

¼ teaspoon sea salt

4 eggs

Grease the inside walls and bottom of five 6-ounce (168 g) ramekins with coconut oil. Prepare a double boiler by setting a glass bowl over a pot of simmering water, but do not let the bowl touch the water. Melt the coconut oil and chocolates in the bowl, stirring together. Remove from the heat and stir in the honey, orange zest, orange juice, and vanilla. Stir in the almond flour and salt. Using an electric mixer, beat in the eggs one at a time, then continue beating for about 3 minutes, until the chocolate turns a slightly lighter shade of brown.

Fill the ramekins until about three-fourths full with batter. Refrigerate for 20 minutes or overnight.

When ready to bake, preheat the oven to 350°F (180°C, or gas mark 4). Place the ramekins on a baking sheet and bake for 12 to 15 minutes, just until the top is set in the center, but still slightly wobbly. You don't want to overcook or you won't have that molten lava center. Remove from the oven and allow to cool slightly. Garnish with additional orange zest. These are best served warm the day they're made.

MAKES 5 CAKES

Gingerbread-Pear Upside-Down Cake

I have to admit one of my favorite parts about this cake, besides the fact that it's gingerbread, is the moment when the pan is lifted from the cake and the beautiful display of pears is revealed. It almost makes you not want to take the first slice. Only kidding ... dive in!

7 Medjool dates, pitted and chopped

5 eggs

⅓ cup (73 g) extra-virgin unrefined coconut oil, melted

¼ cup (61 g) unsweetened applesauce

¼ cup (80 g) unsulfured molasses

½ cup (60 g) coconut flour

1 teaspoon (1.8 g) ground ginger

1 teaspoon (2.3 g) ground cinnamon

1 teaspoon (4.6 g) baking soda

½ teaspoon ground allspice

½ teaspoon unflavored gelatin

½ teaspoon sea salt

2 large ripe pears, cored

4 teaspoons (20 ml) fresh lemon juice

1 teaspoon (5 ml) maple syrup

⅓ cup (45 g) chopped pecans (optional)

Preheat the oven to 350°F (180°C, or gas mark 4). Grease the sides and bottom of a 9-inch (23 cm) round cake pan with coconut oil. Line the bottom with a circle of parchment paper cut to fit. You can do this by tracing the bottom of the pan, then cutting out.

Place the dates in a heat-proof dish. Add enough boiling water to cover the chopped dates, and allow the dates to sit for a few minutes to soften. Drain some of the water, leaving about 1 tablespoon (15 ml), then use a fork to mash the dates until smooth.

In a large bowl, combine the dates, eggs, coconut oil, applesauce, and molasses and mix with a hand mixer until well combine and the dates are incorporated.

In a small bowl, whisk together the coconut flour, ginger, cinnamon, baking soda, allspice, gelatin, and salt. Add the dry ingredients to the wet ingredients and mix together with the hand mixer.

Remove the stems and butts from the cored pears. Cut into halves, then cut each half into 4 wedges. In a mixing bowl, toss together the pears with the lemon, maple syrup, and pecans.

Arrange the pears on the bottom of the prepared cake pan. You can have fun arranging the pears in a pretty pattern. Then pour the cake batter over the pears.

Bake for 20 to 25 minutes, or until golden and a toothpick inserted into the center comes out clean.

Allow the cake to cool for 10 minutes in the pan. Invert a serving plate on top of the pan and, holding the plate and pan together, invert them. Gently pull off the pan, being careful not to burn yourself.

Allow the cake to cool for 10 more minutes before cutting. Best served warm.

The cake can be stored in an airtight container in the refrigerator for up to 3 days.

MAKES ONE 9-INCH (23 CM) CAKE

Cranberry-Citrus Sorbet

This bright red frozen treat spiked with citrus flavors is as beautiful to look at as it is to eat. The tartness of the cranberries marries perfectly with the sweetness of the honey and citrus, making it deliciously refreshing.

12 ounces (336 g) fresh or frozen cranberries

2 cups (470 ml) water

⅓ cup (107 g) raw honey

¼ cup (60 ml) freshly squeezed orange juice

¼ cup (60 ml) freshly squeezed lemon juice

1 tablespoon (6 g) orange zest

¼ teaspoon sea salt

In a medium saucepan over medium-high heat, combine the cranberries, water, honey, orange and lemon juices, orange zest, and salt and cook until the cranberries are soft and bursting, about 15 minutes. Transfer the mixture to a blender or food processor and purée. (Remove the center cap in the blender's lid, or the feed tube from the food processor's lid, and cover the opening with a towel before turning on the machine.) Strain the mixture through a sieve over a bowl to remove the larger bits, then cool completely. Cover with plastic wrap and refrigerate for 2 to 4 hours until completely cold.

Remove the mixture from the refrigerator and pour into the bowl of an ice cream machine. Prepare according to the manufacturer's instructions.

Transfer the sorbet to a freezer-safe container, cover, and freeze the sorbet until hard.

Allow the sorbet to sit at room temperature for 5 to 10 minutes before scooping and serving.

Keep sorbet in the freezer for up to 3 weeks.

MAKES ABOUT 1 PINT (285 G)

Salted Dark Chocolate–Dipped Clementines

I'm like a little kid waiting for the arrival of the box of clementines to hit the market.
These cute little fruits are my favorite of the orange family. They're easy to peel, have no seeds,
and are loved by kids. They are the perfect snack, and dipping them in dark chocolate
and a little salt turns them into a decadent treat.

3 clementines, peeled and segmented

3 ounces (84 g) dark chocolate (90% cacao or unsweetened), chopped

½ teaspoon pink Himalayan salt or sea salt

Line a baking sheet with waxed paper and set aside.

Prepare a double boiler by setting a glass bowl over a pot of simmering water, but do not let the bowl touch the water. Melt the chocolate in the bowl until smooth. Remove from the heat. Dip half of a Clementine segment into the chocolate, coating thoroughly. Rest the segment on the baking sheet. Sprinkle a pinch of salt on the segment—a little goes a long way. As another option, you can also sprinkle with unsweetened shredded coconut.

Once all the segments are dipped and sprinkled, refrigerate until the chocolate is set, about 10 minutes. Serve and enjoy.

Clementine segments can be kept in an airtight container in the refrigerator for up to 2 days.

MAKES 24 TO 30 PIECES

Fruity Coconut Snowballs

These nut-free and no-bake snowballs are quick to assemble and are the perfect complement to a nice hot cup of tea on a cold winter's day.

1¾ cups (140 g) unsweetened shredded coconut, divided

2 teaspoons (9 g) extra-virgin unrefined coconut oil, melted

2 tablespoons (30 ml) canned coconut milk

1 tablespoon (15 ml) maple syrup

2 tablespoons (18 g) unsweetened dried cranberries

1 Medjool date, pitted

1 teaspoon (5 ml) vanilla extract

½ teaspoon ground cinnamon

Pinch of sea salt

Place 1 cup (80 g) of the coconut into the bowl of a food processor along with the coconut oil. Process on high speed, stopping to scrape down the sides of the bowl, until it is a pastelike consistency, 5 to 6 minutes.

Add the coconut milk, maple syrup, cranberries, date, vanilla, cinnamon, and salt and process until well combined. Add ½ cup (40 g) plus 2 tablespoons (10 g) of the coconut and pulse until just combined.

Shape the mixture into twelve 1-inch (2.5 cm) balls and roll in the remaining 2 tablespoons (10 g) coconut. Refrigerate for at least 1 hour and up to 1 week in an airtight container. Best if brought to room temperature before eating.

MAKES 12 SNOWBALLS

Chocolate Cranberry Galette

Galette is a French term that refers to a variety of flat, round cakes, usually made with flaky dough of some kind. This Paleo version has more of a crunchy and crisp crust than that of a traditional flaky pie crust. Use this crust recipe throughout the year and add seasonal fruits to make a variety of galettes.

FOR CRUST:

1½ cups (180 g) almond flour

1 cup (80 g) unsweetened shredded coconut

½ teaspoon ground cinnamon

¼ teaspoon sea salt

¼ cup (55 g) extra-virgin unrefined coconut oil, melted

2 egg yolks

1 tablespoon (15 ml) maple syrup

FOR FILLING:

2 cups (200 g) fresh cranberries

½ cup (60 g) cacao powder

⅓ cup (80 ml) maple syrup

1 tablespoon (14 g) cold ghee or extra-virgin unrefined coconut oil, cut into small pieces

To make the crust: In the bowl of a food processor, combine the almond flour, coconut, cinnamon, and salt and pulse 4 or 5 times until a fine meal forms. Add the coconut oil, egg yolks, and maple syrup and process again until a ball of dough forms. If the dough is still crumbly, add 1 tablespoon (15 ml) water or coconut milk until the dough forms a ball. Wrap the dough in plastic wrap and refrigerate for 1 hour.

Remove the ball of dough from the refrigerator and place on a sheet of parchment paper. Dust the top of the ball with a little coconut flour or almond flour and place another piece of parchment paper even in size on top of the dough. Using a rolling pin, roll the dough into a circle or an oval about ½ inch (1.3 cm) thick. Remove the top layer of parchment paper and transfer the bottom piece of parchment with the dough onto a baking sheet. Return to the refrigerator until you are ready to use.

Preheat the oven to 350°F (180°C, or gas mark 4).

To make the filling: Place the cranberries in a medium bowl and toss with the cacao powder and maple syrup to combine and coat the cranberries.

Pour the cranberry mixture into the center of the dough, leaving room on the sides. Sprinkle the ghee on top of the mixture. Fold the sides of the dough up so it wraps around the fruit, but leaving the very center of the fruit uncovered. If the dough rips, you can patch it up by brushing some water or coconut milk over it and smoothing with your fingers.

Bake for 30 to 35 minutes, or until the dough is golden brown and the filling is bubbling. Remove from the oven and allow to cool before cutting into wedges and serving with a scoop of Vanilla Coconut Ice Cream (page 141), if desired.

The galette is best served the day it is baked.

MAKES 8 SERVINGS

Dark Chocolate–Cranberry Fudge Bars

These no-bake bars are like a fudgy brownie bar that are a bit on the addicting side. My kids love these bars and are happy when I pack them in their lunch boxes for a special treat.

2¼ cup (304 g) pecans, lightly toasted (see Note, page 48)

½ cup (60 g) unsweetened cacao powder

½ teaspoon ground cinnamon

15 Medjool dates, pitted

1 small to medium ripe banana, mashed (about ⅓ cup [75 g])

1 tablespoon (15 ml) vanilla extract

1 tablespoon (20 g) raw honey

¼ cup (38 g) dried cranberries

⅓ cup (58 g) chopped dark chocolate (85% cacao or higher), plus more for garnish

In the bowl of a food processor, blend the pecans, cacao, and cinnamon until combined and coarsely ground.

Add the dates and banana and process until blended. Then add the vanilla and honey and process until well combined.

Stir in the cranberries and chocolate with a spoon or work in by hand.

Press the mixture into an 8 x 8-inch (20 x 20 cm) baking dish and sprinkle with additional chopped dark chocolate, gently pressing down the chocolate bits. Freeze for 1 hour, or until firm, then cut into sixteen 2-inch (5 cm) squares.

The bars are best kept in an airtight container in the refrigerator for up to 6 days.

MAKES 16 SQUARES

♥

chapter seven

ENJOY ALL YEAR:
TREATS USING YEAR–ROUND PRODUCE

By now, I hope you've seen that "baking Paleo" doesn't mean limiting what you can enjoy. Eating seasonally not only celebrates what's readily available at the farmers' markets but also allows us to enjoy food at its most delicious and nutritious. In case the seasonal abundance isn't enough for you, we are fortunate that there is some produce that is naturally available to us year-round. Take pleasure in these seasonless foods any time the mood strikes. But don't forget that there are also nuts, dried fruits, and chocolate that make year-round baking easy and delicious. No matter what season (and what temperature) it may be, the desserts in this chapter will be enjoyed by many.

- **Avocados:** These great-tasting and nutritious foods are filled with heart-healthy monounsaturated fats, which are associated with a reduced risk of heart disease. In addition to being a storehouse of healthy fatty acids, avocados are a concentrated source of fiber, folic acid, vitamin B6, potassium, and copper. Avocados can add creaminess to a dessert, such as in the Chocolate Pudding with Coconut Whipped Cream on page 138. When choosing a ripe, ready-to-eat avocado, it should be slightly soft but should have no dark sunken spots or cracks. The alligator-looking skin should be black, not green. Keep unripe avocados at room temperature. To speed ripening, place in a paper bag with an apple or a banana; to stop ripening, refrigerate for up to 2 days.

- **Bananas:** Wonderfully sweet with firm and creamy flesh, bananas come prepackaged in their own yellow jackets. As bananas ripen they become sweeter in taste, making them perfect to add to a dessert to sweeten naturally. If you are looking to ripen bananas quickly for a recipe, you can place them in a paper bag or wrap them in newspaper, even adding an apple to accelerate the process. If you have ripe bananas on hand but don't have the time to bake, place them in the refrigerator for up to 2 days or the freezer for a month. Keep in mind, even if the peel is darkened it doesn't mean its flesh is affected.

- **Coconut:** This healthy nut-fruit holds a special place in most primal and Paleo hearts. It can be used and enjoyed in many forms, from its milk to its dried flakes, no matter what time of year it is. Try it in Coconut Pecan Chocolate Chunk Cookie Bars (page 142).

Vanilla Cupcakes with Chocolate Frosting

These cupcakes are always on my twin daughters' must-have list when their birthday comes around. Actually, for any birthday—no matter whether it's theirs or not—they request that these be made.

FOR CUPCAKES:

8 large eggs, at room temperature

2 Medjool dates, pitted

½ cup (120 ml) canned coconut milk

½ cup (109 g) extra-virgin unrefined coconut oil, melted

¼ cup (60 ml) maple syrup

1 tablespoon (15 ml) vanilla extract

1 cup (120 g) coconut flour

1 teaspoon (4.6 g) baking soda

½ teaspoon sea salt

FOR CHOCOLATE FROSTING:

1 cup (175 g) chopped dark chocolate (85% cacao or higher)

½ cup (109 g) extra-virgin unrefined coconut oil

1 tablespoon (20 g) raw honey

1 tablespoon (15 ml) vanilla extract

Pinch of sea salt

Preheat the oven to 350°F (180°C, or gas mark 4). Line a 12-cup muffin pan with cupcake liners and set aside.

To make the cupcakes: In the bowl of a food processor, combine the eggs, dates, coconut milk, coconut oil, maple syrup, and vanilla and process until smooth and the dates are completely broken up.

In a small bowl, whisk together the coconut flour, baking soda, and salt. Add the dry ingredients to the wet ingredients and process until fully incorporated.

Remove the blade from the food processor and carefully scoop the batter into the prepared muffin pan. Bake for 30 to 35 minutes, or until golden and a toothpick inserted into the center of one comes out clean.

Allow the cupcakes to cool completely before frosting.

To make the frosting: Prepare a double boiler by setting a glass bowl over a pot of simmering water, but do not let the bowl touch the water. Melt the chocolate and coconut oil in the bowl.

Remove the bowl from the heat once the chocolate has melted and stir in the honey, vanilla, and salt. Stir until smooth. Freeze for about 15 minutes to chill and thicken the chocolate.

Remove from the freezer and, using a hand mixer, whip the frosting until fluffy.

Using a pastry bag, pipe the frosting onto the cooled cupcakes or use a knife to coat the tops of the cupcakes. Top with fresh fruit, if desired.

The cupcakes are best enjoyed the same day they're made but can be kept in the refrigerator in an airtight container for up to 2 days.

MAKES 12 CUPCAKES

Chocolate Pudding with Coconut Whipped Cream

The secret ingredient that gives this pudding a rich texture, similar to traditional dairy puddings, is avocados. Avocados are technically a fruit and are grown year-round in California, which means you can enjoy this chocolate pudding any time you'd like. It is one of my kids' favorite desserts, which makes me happy because they are fueling their little bodies with a nutrient-dense treat as opposed to the other puddings you find at your local grocery store.

FOR CHOCOLATE PUDDING:

2 ripe bananas, mashed

2 ripe avocados

4 Medjool dates, pitted

½ cup (60 g) cacao powder

2 tablespoons (30 ml) canned coconut milk

1 tablespoon (15 ml) maple syrup

1 teaspoon (5 ml) vanilla extract

Dash of sea salt

FOR COCONUT WHIPPED CREAM:

2 cans (13½ ounces, or 400 ml each) coconut milk, refrigerated overnight

1 tablespoon (15 ml) maple syrup

½ teaspoon vanilla extract

Fresh raspberries, for serving

To make the pudding: Place the bananas, avocados, dates, cacao powder, coconut milk, maple syrup, vanilla, and salt into the bowl of a food processor and pulse to combine. Stop to scrape down the sides of the bowl to ensure everything is incorporated.

Scoop the pudding into 4 small serving dishes, cover, and refrigerate for 15 to 20 minutes before serving.

To make the whipped cream: Open the can of coconut without shaking it or turning it upside down. Carefully spoon out the layer of thick coconut cream that has gathered at the top and add it to a mixing bowl.

Add the maple syrup and vanilla along with additional flavorings of choice, such as cinnamon, ginger, or almond extract instead of vanilla. Using a hand mixer, whip the coconut milk until creamy, starting on low and moving to a higher speed. Mix for about 5 minutes, or until you have thick, whipped peaks.

Serve the puddings with the coconut whipped cream and fresh raspberries.

The pudding can be covered and kept in the refrigerator for 2 to 3 days.

MAKES 4 SERVINGS

Vanilla Coconut Ice Cream

This ice cream is a creamy alternative to the traditional vanilla ice cream. It is great served alone or alongside a fruit crumble, such as Peach Berry Spiced Cookie Crumble (page 68), or a brownie, such as Fudgy Chocolate Coffee Brownies (page 155).

1 can (13½ ounces, or 400 ml) coconut milk

¼ cup (60 ml) maple syrup

1 vanilla bean, split lengthwise, seeds scraped, and pod discarded

3 egg yolks

Pinch of sea salt

Combine the coconut milk, maple syrup, vanilla bean seeds, egg yolks, and salt in a medium saucepan. Bring to a low boil over medium heat, whisking constantly, until the mixture thickens and coats the back of a spoon.

Remove the mixture from the heat, strain into a medium bowl, and cover with plastic wrap.

Refrigerate the mixture for 2 hours, or until completely cold. Place the mixture into an ice cream maker and follow the manufacturer's instructions.

Remove the ice cream immediately from the ice cream maker to ensure the ice cream doesn't freeze to the sides. Serve or freeze until ready to enjoy.

Store the ice cream in an airtight container in the freezer for up to 3 weeks.

MAKES 1 PINT (285 G)

Coconut Pecan Chocolate Chunk Cookie Bars

A cookie in a bar, what could be better? Nothing, if you ask my family. These bars were created by raiding my Paleo baking pantry, trying to figure out how to use some ripe bananas sitting on my kitchen counter. For a special treat, my family loves these bars served warm with a scoop of Vanilla Coconut Ice Cream (page 141).

2 ripe bananas, mashed (about 1 cup [225 g])

¼ cup (55 g) extra-virgin unrefined coconut oil, melted

¼ cup (65 g) smooth almond butter

¼ cup (60 ml) maple syrup

¼ cup (56 g) unsweetened applesauce

1 teaspoon (5 ml) vanilla extract

1 cup (80 g) unsweetened shredded coconut

½ cup (60 g) coconut flour

¼ cup (30 g) almond flour

1 teaspoon (2.3 g) ground cinnamon

½ teaspoon baking soda

½ teaspoon sea salt

½ cup (68 g) chopped pecans

1 ounce (28 g) dark chocolate (85% cacao or higher), chopped

1 ounce (28 g) unsweetened dark chocolate, chopped

Preheat the oven to 350°F (180°C, or gas mark 4). Line an 8 x 8-inch (20 x 20 cm) glass baking dish with parchment paper, making sure the paper comes up the sides of the dish.

In a large bowl, add the bananas, coconut oil, almond butter, maple syrup, applesauce, and vanilla. Using a hand mixer, mix the ingredients together until smooth and well combined.

In a small bowl, whisk together the shredded coconut, coconut flour, almond flour, cinnamon, baking soda, and salt.

Add the dry ingredients to the wet ingredients and mix together until incorporated.

Stir in the chopped pecans and chocolate chunks until combined. Pour the batter into the prepared baking dish and spread evenly.

Bake for 35 to 40 minutes, or until the top and sides are golden.

Allow the bars to cool completely before cutting into sixteen 2-inch (5 cm) squares.

The bars can be stored in an airtight container in a cool, dry place for up to 3 days or can be frozen for up to 2 weeks.

MAKES 16 BARS

Banana-Coconut Cream Pie

A creamy banana coconut whipped cream filling cradled in a graham cracker crust topped with fresh banana slices—no wonder this is an ongoing favorite with my friends and family.

FOR CRUST:

14 Graham Crackers (page 160)

2 tablespoons (27 g) extra-virgin unrefined coconut oil, melted

1 tablespoon (15 ml) water

FOR FILLING:

2 cans (13½ ounces, or 400 ml each) coconut milk, refrigerated overnight

1 tablespoon (15 ml) maple syrup

½ teaspoon vanilla extract

2 ripe bananas, mashed

Banana slices, for garnish

Preheat the oven to 350°F (180°C, or gas mark 4).

To make the crust: In the bowl of a food processor, process the graham crackers until finely ground. Add the coconut oil and water and process until the crumbs clump together. Press the mixture into a 9-inch (23 cm) pie plate, pressing up the sides. Place the pie plate on a baking sheet and bake for about 10 minutes, or until slightly golden. Allow the crust to cool completely. To cool quickly, place the crust in the refrigerator or freezer.

To make the filling: Carefully open the cans of coconut milk without shaking or turning them upside down. Spoon out the layer of thick coconut cream that has gathered at the top and add to a mixing bowl. Add the maple syrup and vanilla to the coconut cream and, using a hand mixer, mix everything together until the cream starts to form thick, whipped peaks. Gently fold in the mashed bananas.

Spoon the banana cream mixture into the cooled pie crust, smoothing the top with the back of a spatula. Refrigerate the pie for 30 minutes to allow it to set. Top with the banana slices and serve.

Cover the pie and store in the refrigerator for up to 3 days.

MAKES ONE 9-INCH (23 CM) PIE

Chocolate-Banana-Coconut Freezer Pie

There is nothing like the combination of chocolate and banana, and this pie has them both. It is the perfect anytime treat.

FOR CRUST:

1 cup (80 g) unsweetened shredded coconut

1 cup (135 g) pecan pieces

½ cup (60 g) almond flour

3 tablespoons (24 g) coconut flour

5 Medjool dates, pitted

1 tablespoon (15 ml) maple syrup

1 teaspoon (2.3 g) ground cinnamon

¼ teaspoon sea salt

5 tablespoons (68 g) extra-virgin unrefined coconut oil, melted

⅓ cup (60 g) dark chocolate chips (85% cacao or higher), coarsely chopped

FOR FILLING:

5 small ripe bananas, peeled and broken into small pieces (about 1½ cups [225 g])

¼ cup (30 g) cacao powder

1 cup (235 ml) canned coconut milk

3 tablespoons (45 ml) maple syrup

1 teaspoon (5 ml) vanilla extract

¼ cup (44 g) dark chocolate chunks (85% cacao or higher), coarsely chopped

¼ cup (28 g) sliced almonds, toasted (see Note, page 48)

3 tablespoons (15 g) unsweetened coconut flakes, toasted

1 ounce (28 g) dark chocolate (85% cacao or higher), finely chopped

Preheat the oven to 350°F (180°C, or gas mark 4). Grease a 9-inch (23 cm) springform pan with coconut oil. Set aside.

To make the crust: Place the coconut, pecans, almond flour, coconut flour, dates, maple syrup, cinnamon, and salt into the bowl of a food processor and pulse until the dates are broken up and the mixture looks like loose crumbs. Add the coconut oil and pulse several times in short bursts until the crumbs are moist and begin to fall away from the sides of the bowl. If the dough it too wet, add a bit more almond flour, about 1 tablespoon (8 g) at a time. Remove the blade from the bowl and stir in the dark chocolate chips.

Dump the crumbs into the prepared pan and spread them evenly over the bottom. Using your fingers, gently press the crumbs across the bottom and up the sides, about two-thirds of the way up.

Bake the crust in the center of the oven for about 15 minutes, or until the crust is golden.

Remove the pan and set aside to allow the crust to cool completely.

To make the filling: Combine the bananas, cacao powder, coconut milk, maple syrup, and vanilla in the jar of a blender or food processor. Process until very smooth, like thin cake batter, stopping to scrape down the sides of the jar and stir the mixture to ensure all the bananas are puréed. Stir in the chocolate chunks.

Pour the mixture into the cooled pie crust. Evenly sprinkle the top of the pie with the almonds, coconut, and finely chopped chocolate. Cover very tightly with plastic wrap and freeze for a minimum of 4 hours, or overnight.

To serve, remove the plastic wrap and the springform pan, then let sit at room temperature for about 30 minutes (longer if the pie was frozen for more than 4 hours), until the pie is just soft enough to cut with a knife. Slice and serve.

Cover and store the pie in the freezer for up to 4 weeks. Allow to come to room temperature before cutting and serving.

MAKES ONE 9-INCH (23 CM) PIE

Vanilla Spiced Custard Pie

You will reap the benefits from the coconut in this recipe, which has a low glycemic index, loads of fiber, is rich in medium-chain fatty acids, and is full of vitamins and essential minerals.

FOR CRUST:

2 cups (240 g) almond flour

¼ cup (30 g) cacao powder

¼ teaspoon sea salt

¼ cup (60 ml) maple syrup

¼ cup (55 g) extra-virgin unrefined coconut oil, melted

FOR FILLING:

1 tablespoon (15 ml) water

1½ teaspoons (3.5 g) unflavored gelatin

1 cup (235 ml) canned coconut milk

1 vanilla bean, split lengthwise, seeds scraped, and pod retained

1 cinnamon stick

1 teaspoon whole cloves

3 egg yolks

¼ cup (60 ml) maple syrup

1 cup (225 g) coconut cream (see Note, page 39)

Dark chocolate shavings, for garnish

To make the crust: Grease a 9-inch (23 cm) springform pan with coconut oil.

In a large bowl, combine the almond flour, cacao powder, and salt. Add the maple syrup and coconut oil and blend together with a fork until it resembles a coarse meal, about 2 minutes. Press the dough firmly and evenly into the bottom and halfway up the sides of the prepared pan. Prick the bottom with a fork. Chill the crust in the refrigerator for at least 20 minutes before baking.

When ready to bake, preheat the oven to 350°F (180°C, or gas mark 4).

Bake the crust for 15 to 18 minutes, or until golden but not dark. Remove from the oven and set aside to cool completely. The crust can be made 1 day in advance.

To make the filling: In a small bowl, add the water and sprinkle the gelatin over, without stirring, and set aside.

In a medium saucepan over medium-high heat, heat the coconut milk with the vanilla bean and seeds, cinnamon stick, and cloves for 2 to 3 minutes, or until heated through and fragrant. Strain into a clean bowl.

In a separate medium bowl, whisk together the egg yolks and maple syrup. Slowly pour the coconut milk mixture over the egg mixture, whisking constantly. Return the mixture to the saucepan and heat for 2 to 3 more minutes while whisking, to continue cooking. Pour in the gelatin mixture and whisk until dissolved. Continue heating for 4 to 5 minutes, or until the mixture coats the back of a spoon.

Pour the custard into a bowl and cover the bowl with plastic wrap. Refrigerate for 4 hours or overnight to allow the custard to set. Remove the custard from the refrigerator and pour in the coconut cream. Mix together using a hand mixer until the custard becomes thick and creamy.

Spread the mixture into the crust, cover, and refrigerate for about 30 minutes to 1 hour to allow the custard to set. Remove from the refrigerator, sprinkle the dark chocolate shavings over the top of the pie, and serve.

Cover the pie and store in the refrigerator for up to 3 days.

MAKES ONE 9-INCH (23 CM) PIE

Banana-Coconut Dark Chocolate Squares

When choosing a dark chocolate, reach for 85% cacao and higher. The reason why dark chocolate is so beneficial to your health is because it contains cocoa, which is loaded with polyphenol procyanidins that may protect against heart disease and cancer.

5 Medjool dates, pitted

1 tablespoon (15 ml) water

½ cup (112 g) mashed ripe banana

½ cup (120 ml) canned coconut milk

3 eggs

⅓ cup (73 g) extra-virgin unrefined coconut oil, melted

1½ teaspoons (7.5 ml) vanilla extract

1½ cups (120 g) unsweetened shredded coconut

¼ cup (30 g) coconut flour

¼ teaspoon baking soda

¼ teaspoon sea salt

½ cup (88 g) dark chocolate (85% cacao or higher) chunks

Preheat the oven to 350°F (180°C, or gas mark 4). Grease an 8 x 8-inch (20 x 20 cm) glass baking dish with coconut oil and set aside.

Place the dates into a microwave-safe bowl and add the water. Heat on high for 30 seconds, then mash the dates with a fork.

In the bowl of a food processor, place the banana, coconut milk, dates, eggs, coconut oil, and vanilla and process until the mixture is smooth.

In a large bowl, whisk together the shredded coconut, coconut flour, baking soda, and salt. Pour in the wet ingredients and stir to combine. Add the dark chocolate chunks and stir until evenly incorporated.

Pour the mixture into the prepared baking dish and bake for 25 to 30 minutes, or until golden. Allow the bars to cool completely before cutting into sixteen 2-inch (5 cm) squares.

Keep the squares in an airtight container in the refrigerator.

MAKES 16 SQUARES

Dark Chocolate Cakie Cookies

These are one of my friends' and family's favorite cookies. They're more on the soft side than they are on the crispy. If you prefer your cookies soft, then these are for you!

1 cup (225 g) mashed ripe banana (about 2 bananas)

2 tablespoons (33 g) almond butter

3½ teaspoons (28 g) cacao powder

2 teaspoons (10 ml) vanilla extract

1 teaspoon (4.6 g) baking soda

½ teaspoon ground cinnamon

¼ teaspoon sea salt

1¼ cups (150 g) almond flour

¼ cup (44 g) dark chocolate (85% cacao and higher) chips or chunks

Preheat the oven to 350°F (180°C, or gas mark 4). Line a baking sheet with parchment paper and set aside.

In a large bowl, combine the banana, almond butter, cacao powder, vanilla extract, baking soda, cinnamon, and salt with a hand mixer. Add the almond flour and mix until everything is well combined. Stir the chocolate chips into the batter until well incorporated.

Using an ice cream/cookie scoop, scoop mounds of dough and place on the prepared baking sheet. You can use a small scoop to make more cookies. Bake for 15 minutes, or until the cookies are slightly golden on the bottom and the edges. Allow the cookies to cool on the baking sheet for 5 to 10 minutes, then transfer to a wire rack to cool before handling. The cookies are great once cooled but even better the next day.

Due to their cakelike texture, I prefer to keep these cookies in the refrigerator so they stay fresh longer, but they probably won't last too long.

MAKES 12 LARGE COOKIES OR 24 SMALL COOKIES

Dark Chocolate Almond Cups

My husband's favorite pre-Paleo candy was a peanut butter cup, but I was determined to make a Paleo version so he wouldn't stray on Halloween. These little cups were the result, and he hasn't missed the real thing ever since.

1 cup (175 g) chopped dark chocolate (85% cacao and higher)

½ cup (130 g) almond butter

Prepare a double boiler by setting a glass bowl over a pot of simmering water, but do not let the bowl touch the water. Over very low heat, melt the chocolate in the bowl. Or you can heat the chocolate in the microwave until melted.

With a clean, unused paintbrush, paint the chocolate into a 12-cup candy mold.

Place in the freezer for 10 minutes to allow the chocolate to set. (If not set after 10 minutes, place back in the freezer until the chocolate is solid.)

Fill the hardened chocolate molds with the creamy almond butter.

Rewarm the chocolate over the double boiler, and carefully fill in the top of the mold, over the almond butter, with additional chocolate.

Place in the freezer for 10 to 20 minutes until completely hardened.

Carefully pop the candy out of their molds and serve.

These are best stored in an airtight container in the freezer for up to 2 weeks and brought to room temperature before enjoying.

MAKES 12 CUPS

Snickerdoodle Cookies

When I was growing up, snickerdoodles were one of my favorite cookies that my mom would make during the holiday season. I love cinnamon, and this cookie is all about letting the spice shine. My take on a Paleo version is a soft cookie that has just the right amount of sweetness and spice.

1½ cups (180 g) almond flour

1 tablespoon (8 g) coconut flour

1 teaspoon (2.3 g) ground cinnamon, plus 1 to 2 tablespoons (7 to 14 g) for rolling dough

½ teaspoon ground nutmeg

½ teaspoon baking soda

¼ teaspoon sea salt

1 egg

¼ cup (60 ml) maple syrup

¼ cup (55 g) extra-virgin unrefined coconut oil, melted

1 teaspoon (5 ml) vanilla extract

Preheat the oven to 350°F (180°C, or gas mark 4). Line a baking sheet with parchment paper and set aside.

In a medium bowl, whisk together the almond flour, coconut flour, 1 teaspoon (2.3 g) cinnamon, nutmeg, baking soda, and salt.

In a small bowl, whisk together the egg, maple syrup, coconut oil, and vanilla until well combined. Add the wet ingredients to the dry ingredients and stir to incorporate.

Dust a sheet of waxed paper with 1 tablespoon (7 g) of the ground cinnamon. Using your hands, form a tablespoon-size cookie (about 14 g), and roll it in the cinnamon to coat. Place the cookie on the prepared baking sheet and continue with the remaining dough, making 12 cookies and placing them about 2 inches (5 cm) apart. (Add more of the remaining 1 tablespoon [7 g] cinnamon to the waxed paper, as needed.)

Using the bottom of a cup or a jar, flatten the cookies out into an even thickness.

Bake the cookies for 10 to 12 minutes, or until golden.

Allow the cookies to cool on the baking sheet for 10 minutes, and then transfer to a wire rack to cool completely.

The cookies can be kept in an airtight container in a cool, dry place for up to 2 days.

MAKES 12 COOKIES

Dark Chocolate Cacao Cinnamon Dusted Almonds

These bite-size, chocolate-coated almonds are addicting, I have to warn you. That's why I like to make them and give them away. A perfect holiday gift for those you love.

1½ cups (263 g) chopped dark chocolate

1½ cups (218 g) unsalted roasted almonds

2 tablespoons (16 g) cacao powder

1½ teaspoons (3.5 g) ground cinnamon

Prepare a double boiler by setting a glass bowl over a pot of simmering water, but do not let the bowl touch the water. Over medium-high heat, melt the chocolate in the bowl, stirring the chocolate constantly.

Remove from the heat, add the almonds, and stir until well coated.

Place the almonds on a baking sheet lined with parchment or waxed paper (one that can fit inside your refrigerator).

Refrigerate the almonds for 30 to 60 minutes, or until the chocolate hardens. If you need things to move more quickly, place the chocolate-coated almonds in the freezer.

Place the chocolate-covered almonds in a large bowl and sprinkle with the cacao powder and cinnamon. Toss until well coated.

The almonds can be kept in an airtight container in the refrigerator for 1 to 2 weeks or can be frozen for 1 to 2 months.

MAKES 1½ CUPS (218 G)

Fudgy Chocolate Coffee Brownies

Brownies are my all-time favorite dessert. This fudgy Paleo version will have you surprised they aren't the real ones you used to enjoy in your pre-Paleo days. If you have little ones in the house and don't want them to have the coffee, you can replace the brewed coffee with coconut milk and eliminate the ground coffee.

6 Medjool dates, pitted

3 eggs

½ cup (112 g) unsweetened applesauce

⅓ cup (73 g) extra-virgin unrefined coconut oil, melted

2 tablespoons (30 ml) canned coconut milk

2 tablespoons (33 g) almond butter

1 tablespoon (15 ml) freshly brewed coffee

1 tablespoon (20 g) raw honey

1 teaspoon (5 ml) vanilla extract

2 ounces (56 g) unsweetened dark chocolate (100% cacao), melted (see Note)

3 tablespoons (24 g) coconut flour

2 tablespoons (16 g) cacao powder

½ teaspoon freshly ground coffee beans

¼ teaspoon baking soda

¼ teaspoon gluten-free baking powder (see page 21 for a homemade version)

¼ teaspoon sea salt

1 ounce (28 g) dark chocolate (85% or higher), chopped

Preheat the oven to 350°F (180°C, or gas mark 4). Line a glass 8 x 8-inch (20 x 20 cm) baking dish with parchment paper, allowing the paper to come up the sides.

In the bowl of a food processor, combine the dates, eggs, applesauce, coconut oil, coconut milk, almond butter, brewed coffee, honey, and vanilla and process until smooth. Add the melted unsweetened chocolate and process again until the chocolate is incorporated.

In a small bowl, whisk together the coconut flour, cacao powder, coffee beans, baking soda, baking powder, and salt. Add the dry ingredients to the wet ingredients and process again until everything is incorporated. Remove the blade from the food processor and stir in the chopped dark chocolate.

Pour the brownie batter into the prepared baking dish, spreading evenly. Bake for 20 to 25 minutes. A toothpick inserted into the center should come out wet with moist batter sticking to it. You want to make sure not to overcook the brownies or they will be dry and not fudgy.

Allow the brownies to cool completely before slicing into sixteen 2-inch (5 cm) squares.

The brownies can be kept in an airtight container in the refrigerator for up to 4 days or frozen for up to 2 months. If frozen, allow the bars to come to room temperature before enjoying.

MAKES 16 BROWNIES

𝓝ote: To melt the chocolate, chop it and place in a microwave-safe glass bowl. Microwave on high for 30 seconds, stir, then microwave again for 15 seconds. Repeat until the chocolate is melted and smooth.

Pinwheel Cookies

In my house, I barely can get these out of the oven and cooled before the hands
are reaching for them.

2 eggs

3 Medjool dates, pitted

½ cup (109 g) extra-virgin unrefined coconut oil, melted

¼ cup (60 ml) maple syrup

1 teaspoon (5 ml) vanilla extract

3 cups (360 g) almond flour

1 teaspoon (4.6 g) baking soda

½ teaspoon sea salt

¼ cup (30 g) cacao powder

1 egg white

In the bowl of a food processor, combine the eggs, dates, coconut oil,
maple syrup, and vanilla and process until smooth and the dates are
completely broken up.

In a small bowl, whisk together the almond flour, baking soda, and
salt. Add the dry ingredients to the wet ingredients and combine.

Divide the dough in half, keeping one half in the food processor and
the other half in a separate bowl. Add the cacao powder to the
dough in the food processor and pulse to allow the cacao powder
to completely incorporate into the dough.

Gather each portion of dough into a ball and wrap separately in plastic
wrap. Refrigerate for 45 to 60 minutes.

In a small bowl, use a fork to beat the egg white until foamy.

Remove the dough from the refrigerator. One at a time, dust the
dough with almond flour, place each dough portion between 2 sheets
of waxed paper, and roll out into a rectangle about ¼-inch (6 mm)
thick. Remove the top piece of waxed paper from each rectangle.
Brush the egg white lightly over the top surface of the chocolate
dough. Using the waxed paper, flip the chocolate dough onto the
vanilla dough and press the dough together. Peel off and discard the
top piece of waxed paper. Trim the dough edges evenly. Refrigerate
the dough for 10 to 20 minutes, until the dough can be handled.

Remove the dough from the refrigerator and roll up the two layers
into a tight log, removing the remaining piece of waxed paper as you
roll. Trim the ends evenly. Wrap in plastic wrap and refrigerate until
firm, at least 1 hour or overnight.

Preheat the oven to 350°F (180°C, or gas mark 4). Line a baking
sheet with parchment paper. Using a sharp knife, cut the dough
crosswise into 18 disks ¼-inch (6 mm) thick. Place them 1 inch (2.5
cm) apart on the prepared baking sheet and bake for 8 to 12 minutes,
or until golden around the edges. Cool on the baking sheet for 5 to 10
minutes, and transfer them to a wire rack to cool completely.

The cookies should be stored in an airtight container in the refrigerator
for up to 4 days or frozen for up to 60 days. Just bring to room
temperature before enjoying.

MAKES 18 COOKIES

S'Mores

S'mores are a summertime favorite, but they are also great when the temperatures cool down. There is nothing better than biting into the crunch of the graham cracker and tasting the combo of marshmallow and chocolate.

FOR MARSHMALLOWS:

½ **cup (120 ml) cold water, divided**

1½ **tablespoons (12 g) unflavored gelatin**

¼ **cup (80 g) raw honey**

⅛ **teaspoon sea salt**

½ **teaspoon vanilla extract**

32 **Graham Crackers (page 160)**

16 **squares dark chocolate (70% cacao and higher)**

To make the marshmallows: Lightly grease an 8 x 8-inch (20 x 20 cm) baking pan with coconut oil. Line the pan with parchment paper, with enough to hang over the edges of the pan, and then grease the parchment paper with coconut oil. *Optional:* To ensure the marshmallows do not stick to the parchment, you can add ⅓ cup (27 g) unsweetened shredded coconut to the bottom of the pan.

Pour ¼ cup (60 ml) of the water into the bowl of a stand mixer fitted with the whisk attachment and sprinkle the gelatin over the water. Set aside to soften.

In a small saucepan over medium heat, combine the honey, remaining ¼ cup (60 ml) water, and salt, whisking to combine. Simmer gently until the syrup reaches 240°F (116°C) on a candy thermometer.

With the mixer on medium speed, very slowly add the hot honey mixture to the gelatin and water. This should take about 2 minutes to add all of the honey mixture. Then add the vanilla and blend to incorporate. Turn the mixer on high and blend for 10 minutes, until the mixture doubles and becomes light and fluffy. Pour into the prepared pan, then place another piece of greased parchment on top and press down to smooth into an even layer. Allow the marshmallow to sit at room temperature overnight, uncovered.

The next day, flip the marshmallow onto a greased cutting board. Cut into sixteen 2-inch (5 cm) squares, using a knife lightly greased with coconut oil. Also grease your hands with coconut oil to keep the marshmallow from sticking to them.

To assemble, place a graham cracker face down, top with a marshmallow and a dark chocolate square, and top with an additional graham cracker. You can also lightly toast the marshmallows before adding to the s'more, but keep in mind that they won't toast like the marshmallows you are accustomed to. They will become gooey and soft and won't burn. Also, it won't take long for them to soften, so watch them carefully if toasting.

Any leftover marshmallows are best stored in an airtight container at room temperature.

MAKES 16 S'MORES

Graham Crackers

My kids loved graham crackers prior to our Paleo days. These are pretty close to those store-bought graham crackers they once loved but without hidden additives, gluten, and sugar. These graham crackers can be enjoyed on their own, crushed for a pie crust, or used for S'mores (page 159).

1¾ cups (210 g) almond flour

¼ cup (30 g) hazelnut flour

¼ cup (30 g) coconut flour

¾ teaspoon unflavored gelatin

3 Medjool dates, pitted and chopped

1 tablespoon (20 g) raw honey

½ teaspoon baking soda

¼ teaspoon ground cinnamon

¼ teaspoon sea salt

3 tablespoons (42 g) ghee, cut into pieces

2 tablespoons (28 g) extra-virgin unrefined coconut oil, in solid form, cut into pieces

2 tablespoons (30 ml) canned coconut milk

1½ tablespoons (30 g) unsulfured molasses

½ teaspoon vanilla extract

Preheat the oven to 350°F (180°C, or gas mark 4).

In the bowl of a food processor, place the almond flour, hazelnut flour, coconut flour, gelatin, dates, honey, baking soda, cinnamon, and salt and pulse to combine. Add the ghee and coconut oil and pulse again until the mixture becomes a soft crumble. Add the coconut milk, molasses, and vanilla and process until the dough forms a ball. The dough will be tacky.

Place the dough on a large piece of parchment paper and dust the top with a little coconut flour. Place another equally large piece of parchment paper on top of the dough and gently press down. Using a rolling pin, roll the dough out between the parchment papers until it is a rectangle about 14 x 10 inches (35.5 x 25.5 cm) and ⅛- to ¼-inch (3 to 6 mm) thick. Remove the top layer of parchment paper. Using a pizza cutter, cut the dough into thirty-five 2-inch (5 cm) squares, but do not separate them. Using a fork, poke holes in the top of the dough. Leave the graham crackers on the parchment paper and transfer to a baking sheet.

Bake the graham crackers for 15 to 20 minutes, rotating the baking sheet halfway through the baking time. The crackers will be ready when the edges just start to turn golden. Remove them from the oven and cool completely. When the crackers are completely cooled, carefully break into individual squares using the cuts you made prior to baking.

They should be stored in an airtight container at room temperature for up to 5 days. You can also freeze these cookies for up to 2 months.

MAKES 35 COOKIES

Chocolate Whoopie Pies with Vanilla Cream

Fun fact on whoopie pies: Rumor has it that these treats were packed in the lunch boxes of Amish school children. They would open their lunch boxes, spot the treats, and shout, "Whoopie!" Funny thing is, my kids do the same thing.

FOR WHOOPIE PIES:

5 eggs

½ cup (120 ml) canned coconut milk

½ cup (109 g) extra-virgin unrefined coconut oil, melted

⅓ cup (80 ml) maple syrup

2 tablespoons (33 g) almond butter

1 tablespoon (15 ml) vanilla extract

½ cup (60 g) coconut flour

¼ cup (30 g) cacao powder

1 teaspoon (4.6 g) baking soda

½ teaspoon sea salt

FOR VANILLA CREAM:

2 cans (13½ ounces, or 400 ml each) coconut milk, refrigerated overnight

1 tablespoon (15 ml) maple syrup

1 teaspoon (5 ml) vanilla extract

Preheat the oven to 350°F (180°C, or gas mark 4). Grease a 12-cup whoopie pie pan with coconut oil. If you don't have a whoopie pie pan you can also use a 12-cup muffin pan.

To make the whoopie pies: In a large bowl, whisk together the eggs, coconut milk, coconut oil, maple syrup, almond butter, and vanilla until well combined.

In a small bowl, whisk together the coconut flour, cacao powder, baking soda, and salt. Add the dry ingredients to the wet ingredients and stir to combine until everything is incorporated.

Carefully pour the batter into the prepared pan, making sure not to fill to the rim. If using a muffin pan, fill the cups only one-third full. The size and look of your whoopie pies will be slightly different when using the muffin pan.

Bake for 22 to 25 minutes, or until a toothpick inserted into the center of a whoopie pie comes out clean. Allow the whoopie pies to cool in the pan for 10 to 15 minutes before releasing them from the pan. Transfer to a wire rack and cool completely.

To make the cream: Remove the coconut milk from the refrigerator and carefully open the cans without shaking or turning them upside down. Carefully spoon out the layer of thick coconut cream that has gathered at the top and add to a mixing bowl.

Add the maple syrup and vanilla to the coconut cream and blend together with a hand mixer, starting on low and moving to a higher speed, until creamy. Then mix for about 5 minutes, or until you have thick, whipped peaks.

Carefully cut the whoopie pies in half. On the top of the bottom half of one of the pies, place a dollop of cream and gently press the top half on top of the cream, spreading the cream to the edges of the pie. The pies are best served immediately but can be kept in an airtight container in the refrigerator for up to 2 days.

MAKES 12 WHOOPIE PIES

Spiced Cookie Cutter Cookies

During the holidays when I was growing up, my favorite cookies to help my mom with were the ones I got to cut out. When making the switch to a Paleo lifestyle, I was determined to find an alternative to the cookie cutter cookies I grew up with. It took some trial and error, but now my daughters can experience the fun of cutting out their own cookies.

1¾ cups (210 g) almond flour

2 tablespoons (28 g) extra-virgin unrefined coconut oil, in solid form

2 tablespoons (30 ml) maple syrup

1 Medjool date, pitted and chopped

1 tablespoon (15 ml) canned coconut milk

1 teaspoon (5 ml) vanilla extract

1 teaspoon (2.3 g) ground cinnamon

½ teaspoon ground ginger

⅛ teaspoon cloves

½ teaspoon baking soda

½ teaspoon unflavored gelatin

Pinch of sea salt

Preheat the oven to 350°F (180°C, or gas mark 4). Line a baking sheet with parchment paper and set aside.

In the bowl of a food processor, add the almond flour, coconut oil, maple syrup, date, coconut milk, vanilla, cinnamon, ginger, cloves, baking soda, gelatin, and salt and process until a dough comes together and forms a ball.

Dust a piece of parchment paper with coconut flour. Place the dough on the parchment paper and dust with additional coconut flour. Place another piece of parchment paper on top of the dough and roll out the dough to ¼-inch (6 mm) thick. Remove the top layer of parchment paper. Cut out 12 cookies with your cookie cutter of choice and carefully place on the prepared baking sheet. Re-roll the dough and cut out more cookies. Bake the cookies for 10 to 12 minutes, rotating the pan halfway through, or until golden around the edges.

Allow the cookies to cool for 5 to 10 minutes on the baking sheet before transferring to a wire rack to cool completely.

The cookies are best kept in an airtight container in a cool, dry place for up to 3 days.

MAKES 12 COOKIES

Note: To decorate the cookies, you can use dark chocolate chips (with no additives), unsweetened shredded coconut, or chopped nuts. You can also melt dark chocolate and drizzle it over the cookies. Let your imagination make magic when decorating.

Marbled Chocolate Banana Mini Cakes

These cakes can easily be made into a larger cake by just opting for a larger pan such as a Bundt cake pan or a loaf pan. To ensure you get the beautiful marble look, don't over swirl the banana and chocolate batters together.

1½ cups (338 g) mashed ripe bananas (about 3 bananas)

¼ cup (60 ml) maple syrup

1 tablespoon (15 ml) vanilla extract

4 eggs

½ cup (109 ml) extra-virgin unrefined coconut oil, melted

¼ cup (60 ml) canned coconut milk

½ cup (60 g) coconut flour

1 teaspoon (4.6 g) baking soda

1 teaspoon (2.3 g) ground cinnamon

½ teaspoon sea salt

3 tablespoons (24 g) cacao powder

2 ounces (56 g) dark chocolate (85% cacao or higher), melted (optional)

Preheat the oven to 350°F (180°C, or gas mark 4). Grease a 6-cup mini cake pan with coconut oil and dust with coconut flour.

In a large bowl using a hand mixer, mix together the bananas, maple syrup, vanilla, eggs, coconut oil, and coconut milk until smooth.

In a small bowl, whisk together the coconut flour, baking soda, cinnamon, and salt. Add the dry ingredients to the wet ingredients and blend with the hand mixer.

Divide the batter in half, in 2 bowls. To one half of the batter, add the cacao powder and blend with the hand mixer until incorporated.

Spoon the batter, alternating one scoop of banana batter and one scoop of chocolate batter, into the mini cake pans. Continue to alternate the batter in the pan to almost form a pattern in the pan. To create marbling, run a toothpick or a table knife through the batters in a swirling motion, making sure not to over swirl the batter.

Bake for 30 to 40 minutes, rotating the pan halfway through, until a toothpick inserted into the center of one comes out clean. Transfer the pan to a rack to cool for 10 minutes. Turn the cakes out from the pan and cool completely on a rack.

Drizzle the melted dark chocolate over the cakes.

The cakes can be kept in an airtight container at room temperature for up to 3 days.

MAKES 6 CAKES

RESOURCES

You can obtain many of the ingredients in this book from your local health food store and better grocery stores, but you may need other resources from time to time. Listed here are some of my favorite online places to find ingredients that are Paleo-friendly. The purveyors at your local farmers' market are required to submit safety records that are in compliance with local, state, and federal regulations—particularly when it comes to meat and dairy. But, when buying directly from the farm, make sure you have done your research and that your purchases are from a safe and reliable source.

GRAIN-FREE FLOURS

Almond Flour and Almond Meal

Honeyville Grain Blanched Almond Flour and Almond Meal: www.honeyvillegrain.com

Coconut Flour

Coconut Secret Raw Organic Coconut Flour: www.coconutsecret.com

Hazelnut Flour

King Arthur Flour: www.kingarthurflour.com

FATS AND OILS

Coconut Oil

Wilderness Family Naturals: www.wildernessfamilynaturals.com
Tropical Traditions: www.tropicaltraditions.com

Ghee

Pure Indian Foods 100% Organic Grass-Fed Ghee: www.pureindianfoods.com
Purity Farms Organic Ghee: www.purityfarms.com

SWEETENERS

Honey

Raw Honey: www.reallyrawhoney.com

Maple Syrup

Maple Valley Organic Grade B Maple Syrup: www.maplevalleysyrup.com
Shady Maple Farms Organic Grade A Maple Syrup: www.abesmarket.com

OTHER ESSENTIALS

Cacao Powder

Rapunzel Organic Cocoa Powder: www.tropicaltraditions.com

Wilderness Family Naturals: www.wildernessfamilynaturals.com

Coconut Milk

Native Forest Organic Coconut Milk: www.edwardandsons.com

Dark Chocolate

Alter Eco Fair Trade 85% Dark Chocolate: www.alterecofoods.com

Askinosie 77% Dark Chocolate Bar: www.askinosie.com

SunSpire 100% Dark Chocolate: www.sunspire.com

Theo Chocolate Company 85% Dark Chocolate Bar: www.chocosphere.com

Gelatin

Bernard Jensen's Grass Fed Unflavored Gelatin: www.amazon.com

Organic Nuts

Nuts.com: www.nutsonline.com

RECOMMENDED PALEO WEBSITES

Against All Grain: www.againstallgrain.com

Balanced Bites: www.balancedbites.com

Foodee: www.thefoodee.com

The Food Lovers Primal Palate: www.primal-palate.com

Health-Bent: www.health-bent.com

Multiply Delicious: www.multiplydelicious.com

Nom Nom Paleo: www.nomnompaleo.com

PaleOMG: www.paleomg.com

Paleo Parents: www.paleoparents.com

Robb Wolf: www.robbwolf.com

The Urban Poser: www.urbanposer.blogspot.com

ABOUT THE AUTHOR

Heather Connell is a busy mom to twin daughters and the voice and creator of Multiply Delicious, a blog where she shares her passion for cooking and baking Paleo. Heather was introduced to Paleo after suffering health issues of her own. With diet alone she regained her health and hasn't looked back. She is now a certified Holistic Nutritionist and is committed to educating others on how Paleo can help them live a healthier lifestyle. Paleo changed her life, and she is using the knowledge she has gained inside and outside the kitchen to help families implement Paleo successfully into their lives.

ACKNOWLEDGMENTS

This might be the hardest part of the book for me. There are so many people who have influenced me over the years and led me to where I am today. I am truly blessed to have these people in my life. I would love to mention everyone, but because I can't, here is a list of people who have made this book possible.

First and foremost, to my husband Scott, thank you for your love and encouragement. I couldn't have done this without your help managing our family while I typed, tested, photographed, and cooked for three months straight. This book never would have come to be without you. Thank you for being my taste tester and telling me your honest opinion. You are an extraordinary person, and I'm so lucky I get to share my life with you.

To my little girls Clair and Laine, I can't even begin to tell you how much I love and adore you both. You have been my little helpers throughout this cookbook journey, be it tasting recipes and giving me a thumbs-up or -down to helping me measure and mix, all while smiling and giggling. Your spirit and excitement drove me forward.

To Mom, what can I say? Beginning when I was a little girl you taught me your culinary craft. Even though it took me getting married to actually fall in love with cooking, I will forever be grateful for those times spent in the kitchen as a child by your side. Outside the kitchen your support, love, encouragement, and guidance have shaped me. Thank you for believing in me every step of the way. You will never know how thankful I am of you.

To my in-laws, Dennis and Nancy, thank you for your support, help, encouragement, and love. Our family is truly blessed because you are in it.

To my Metro Crossfit family, thank you for cheering me on, not only as I sweat every day but also on my journey with the cookbook. You have been amazing taste testers, and I am forever grateful for your help.

To my editor, Jill Alexander at Fair Winds Press, you have been my long-distance tour guide to book writing. You never compromised quality at any point—only asking what will make this book better. It has been a joy working with you. Thank you for believing in me and making a dream of mine come true.

To Becca Bond Photography, thank you for capturing the perfect images of me and the girls in the kitchen. I will cherish those images forever. You are a true talent!

Finally, thank you to each and every one of my blog readers. Your constant support and comments keep me going and make what I do on the blog so special. It is a true joy to continue to create new recipes for you to use in your homes.

INDEX